VEGGIENOMICS

VEGGIE NOMICS

Thrifty meat-free cooking at its best

VEGGIENOMICS

Thrifty meat-free cooking at its best

★ Nicola Graimes ★

NOURISH
EAT WELL, LIVE WELL

Veggienomics
Nicola Graimes

First published in the United Kingdom and Ireland
in 2014 by Nourish, an imprint of
Watkins Publishing Limited
PO Box 883, Oxford, OX1 9PL

A member of Osprey Group
enquiries@nourishbooks.com

Publisher: Grace Cheetham
Project Manager: Rebecca Woods
Editor: Liz Jones
Managing Designer: Suzanne Tuhrim
Commissioned Photography: Toby Scott
Food Stylist: Jayne Cross
Prop Stylist: Lucy Harvey
Illustrator: Cecilia Carey
Production: Uzma Taj

A CIP record for this book is available from the
British Library

ISBN: 978-1-84899-169-9

10 9 8 7 6 5 4 3 2 1

Typeset in Block Dog, Thirsty Rough and Univers
Colour reproduction by PDQ UK
Printed in China

Notes on the Recipes
Unless otherwise stated:
- Use medium eggs, fruit and vegetables
- Use fresh ingredients, including herbs and spices
- Do not mix metric and imperial measurements
- 1 tsp = 5ml   1 tbsp = 15ml   1 cup = 250ml

Publisher's Note
While every care has been taken in compiling the
recipes for this book, Watkins Publishing Limited,
or any other persons who have been involved
in working on this publication, cannot accept
responsibility for any errors or omissions,
inadvertent or not, that may be found in the recipes
or text, nor for any problems that may arise as
a result of preparing one of these recipes. If you
are pregnant or breastfeeding or have any special
dietary requirements or medical conditions, it is
advisable to consult a medical professional before
following any of the recipes contained in this book.

Watkins Publishing Limited is supporting the
Woodland Trust, the UK's leading woodland
conservation charity, by funding tree-planting
initiatives and woodland maintenance.

www.nourishbooks.com

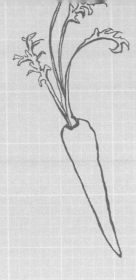

Contents

Introduction 6

Basics and Accompaniments 12

1.

Tin of Beans (and Other Pulses) 26

2.

Pack of Pasta (and Noodles) 44

3.

Sack of Rice (and Other Grains) 66

4.

Bag of Nuts (and Seeds) 88

5.

Carton of Eggs 110

6.

Slice of Cheese (and Other Dairy) 130

7.

Box of Veg 152

Index 174

Acknowledgements 176

Introduction

In my previous cookbook, *New Vegetarian Kitchen*, the focus was on experimenting with cooking techniques and ingredients in an adventurous way; playing around with flavours, colours and textures to create a collection of contemporary recipes that utilize the amazing range of foods now available to us. *Veggienomics* pares things back with a series of recipes that are in tune with the demands of today's home cook: straightforward, simple dishes that don't compromise on good taste, are nutritious and, importantly, don't burn a hole in your pocket.

We are all increasingly aware of the price of food and the environmental cost and inefficiencies of producing meat on a large scale, which is why cooking vegetarian – whether 100 per cent or the occasional meal – makes both economic and environmental sense. Additionally, most of us don't have much time to spend shopping or cooking on a daily basis. *Veggienomics* helps you to plan ahead (making the most of what you've got is crucial when you're on a budget), with advice on shopping, stocking the storecupboard, making the most of your freezer, using up leftovers, menu planning, growing your own fresh produce and even foraging for free.

Here is a collection of recipes that make use of storecupboard staples such as beans, pulses, pasta, rice, noodles and grains as well as nuts, cheese, dairy and eggs, supplemented with fresh vegetables – be they shop-bought, homegrown or foraged.

I've taken a back-to-basics approach, with recipes for making your own stock, spice mix, soft cheese, yogurt, preserves, pickles and syrups, as well as sprouting your own beans. These aren't just fun and easy to do, but they also make economic sense – these foods can be pricey to buy. Some figures suggest that in the West we throw away as much as a third of the food we buy – which is why it makes sense to make the most of the food we have by using the freezer, and cooking with leftovers (even just a crust of bread, cheese rind or some surplus cooked veg).

Geared to our busy lives and varying culinary demands, each chapter in the book includes recipes and suggestions for snacks, lunches and dinners. There are also suggestions for matching recipes if you are cooking a whole meal. Where a recipe uses a slightly more unusual ingredient, an alternative is given in case you can't find it. I also like to use the same ingredient in a few recipes so you aren't left with a bottle of something languishing in the cupboard.

My original plan for *Veggienomics* centred around clever shopping and making the most of the weekly shop, but then it blossomed into something wider to include growing your own fresh produce and foraging, both favourite pastimes of mine. This book isn't about living off the land à la *The Good Life* – rather it is intended to give you a taste of what's feasible from a small plot, or by discovering your local environment.

I wouldn't say I'm a big-time gardener, but I like to grow a selection of veg and herbs at home and share an allotment with a few friends, where we have had a good rate of success. It's not only immensely satisfying, but also extremely therapeutic when you spend much of your time in front of a computer. Similarly, my interest in foraging was initially spurred on after finding some spectacular porcini mushrooms – it doesn't get much better than that!

So if you want to cut down on the amount of meat you eat on a weekly basis (or even cut it out of your diet altogether), and watch what you spend on your weekly shop, I hope that you will agree that *Veggienomics* includes recipes to inspire … without costing the earth.

STOCKING THE STORECUPBOARD

Storecupboard ingredients form the cornerstone of the recipes. You'll find that you have the foundations of many good meals, and only have to buy the fresh ingredients to supplement them.

If you eat pasta, rice, beans and lentils on a weekly basis it makes economic sense to buy them in bulk. If you don't eat them regularly enough to buy large quantities for yourself, share large bags with family and friends. It's also possible to buy some dried foods in loose form, meaning you can buy exactly the amount you need and don't have to pay for fancy packaging.

Rice and Grains

A staple food for over half the world's population, rice features in many cuisines: think Italian risotto, Spanish paella and Middle Eastern pilaffs, not forgetting Asian food.

The two main ways to cook rice are the open boiling method, where you cover the rice with plenty of water then drain it when cooked, and the absorption method. I tend to go for the latter, as taught to me by the rice connoisseur Sri Owen, as I find it gives perfectly cooked, fluffy rice.

To cook long-grain rice for four people by the absorption method, thoroughly rinse 200g/7oz/1 cup rice to remove excess starch. Put the rice in a saucepan and cover with double the volume of water and ½ tsp salt (the water should be about 1cm/½in above the top of the rice). Bring to the boil, uncovered, then turn the heat down to its lowest setting, cover with a lid and simmer for 10 minutes, or until the water has been absorbed and the rice is tender. Remove the pan from the heat and leave to stand, covered, for 5 minutes. Fluff up the grains with a fork before serving.

While rice, in its many forms, reigns supreme in the world of grains, there are so many more types to choose from when stocking a storecupboard: barley, bulgur wheat, couscous, buckwheat, oats, polenta and quinoa are all worthy of mention and inexpensive. Barley is great in hearty soups and stews, and also makes a good alternative to rice in risotto and paella. I like to use protein-rich quinoa, or buckwheat, bulgur or couscous, to serve with tagines and stews as well as in salads and pilaffs. Polenta and oats make a lovely crispy crust for fritters, croquettes and burgers.

Pasta and Noodles

Long or short, thick or thin, smooth or ridged, curly or straight – there is a plethora of shapes and sizes of dried pasta to choose from. The choice may feel intimidating, but the general 'rule' is that the pasta shape should work in harmony with the accompanying sauce. Perfect pasta pairings include thin, long pasta such as spaghetti and linguine with olive oil-based sauces, and thicker strands with cream and tomato sauces, while heavy, chunky sauces require a sturdier, shorter shape such as rigatoni or penne. Ridged or curly shapes are good for 'capturing' sauces, giving them something to cling on to. It makes sense to have a varied selection – but then again you don't want too many open bags, containing not enough pasta to make a decent-sized meal!

When cooking pasta, immerse it (a decent serving is 100g/3½oz/heaped 1 cup dried pasta per person) in plenty of boiling water to prevent it sticking. Salt the water generously (about 1 tablespoon per 1l/35fl oz/4 cups); the water should be as salty as the sea. Stir the pasta occasionally to prevent it sticking, and keep the water at a rolling boil. When draining pasta, reserve a little of the cooking water to loosen the accompanying sauce if necessary.

While noodles also come in a range of lengths and thicknesses, it tends to be the type of grain used, rather than the shape, that defines how they are cooked and served. Egg noodles and chunky udon work in stir-fries, while lighter rice and soba noodles suit soupy broths and Asian salads.

Beans and Lentils

Dried beans and lentils are storecupboard essentials in my kitchen. Extremely economical and nutritious, it pays to buy them in bulk if they are a regular part of your diet. Look for smooth, plump dried beans, and store them in an airtight container in a cool, dark cupboard where they'll keep for up to a year. Keep an eye on the use-by date, as beans become tough when old.

Don't dismiss tinned beans and lentils, as they make a convenient addition to the storecupboard for when you don't have time or the inclination to soak and cook dried ones. I like to use them in speedy lunchtime salads or warming pan-fries and, as they tend to be softer in texture than cooked dried beans, they are great in pâtés, stuffings, croquettes and fritters.

The relevant recipes in this book give the weight of both drained tinned beans and dried cooked beans. Remember that dried beans double their weight when cooked: 100g/3½oz/½ cup borlotti beans will produce 200g/7oz/1 cup cooked borlotti. A standard 400g/14oz tin of chickpeas will contain both the chickpeas and brine, so you need to keep an eye on the drained weight given on the label: for instance, a 400g/14oz tin will contain roughly 235g/8½oz/heaped 1½ cups chickpeas.

Back to dried beans. With a few exceptions they will cook more quickly and evenly if pre-soaked for 6–8 hours in plenty of cold water. If time is short, you can try the quick-soak method: cook the beans in boiling water for 2 minutes, then remove the pan from the heat, cover and leave for 1 hour until cold. Whichever method you use, drain and rinse them before cooking. Dried lentils and mung beans don't need pre-soaking, but you should rinse them well before cooking.

To cook dried beans and lentils, put them in a saucepan and cover with plenty of cold water, cover, and bring to the boil. (If cooking dried kidney beans it is essential that you boil them for 10 minutes to destroy the toxins.) Turn the heat down, part-cover the pan and gently boil, stirring occasionally, until the beans are tender. Salt the cooking water about three-quarters of the way through cooking to avoid toughening the beans. Also, check the pan occasionally to make sure there is enough water and top up if necessary. Cooking times will vary depending on the age of the beans or lentils, but use the following table as a guideline (a pressure cooker will reduce the time by around three-quarters).

	Pre-soaking	Cooking time
BEANS		
Aduki beans	yes	45 minutes
Black beans	yes	1–1½ hours
Borlotti beans	yes	1–1½ hours
Butter (lima) beans	yes	1 hour
Cannellini beans	yes	1–1½ hours
Chickpeas	yes	1–2 hours
Fava (broad) beans (split)	yes	40 minutes–1 hour
Flageolet beans	yes	1–1½ hours
Haricot beans	yes	1–1½ hours
Kidney beans	yes	1½ hours
Mung beans	no	45 minutes
Pinto beans	yes	1–1½ hours
Soya beans	yes	2–3 hours
LENTILS		
Green lentils	no	30 minutes–45 minutes
Puy lentils	no	30 minutes–45 minutes
Red split lentils	no	25 minutes

FILLING THE FRIDGE

Much of the food that tends to be thrown away is chilled, so it pays to be mindful when stocking the fridge to avoid wastage. When shopping for food, take a list (with a rough breakdown of the week's meals) – this will help to keep you focused and avoid making unwanted impulse purchases that won't be used. To ensure that chilled foods last as long as they should, store them correctly in the fridge. Make sure your fridge is energy efficient and set at 4–5°C (40–41°F), and be conscious of 'best before' or 'eat by' dates. Make sure food is wrapped or covered to avoid cross-contamination and the transfer of smells from strong cheese, garlic or spring onions, for instance. Many say that eggs don't have to be stored in the fridge if you have a cool place to keep them, but when the weather is warm it's sensible to put them in the door of the fridge. Similarly, the bottom of the fridge or the salad drawer are the perfect temperature for uncooked vegetables and salad leaves.

USING THE FREEZER

Freezing is a useful way to preserve food, extending its shelf-life and enabling you to make the most of leftovers and gluts of fresh produce. Make meals in bulk and freeze the surplus. Also, leftover ends of bread are perfect for turning into breadcrumbs and freezing in pots – they are usable from frozen.

A full freezer costs less to run than a half-empty one, so it pays to make the most of the space, but remember that food that is past its best is not improved by freezing. Keep the freezer at –18°C (–0.4°F) or below, as at this temperature food pathogens and harmful micro-organisms are dormant. For best results, freeze home-cooked foods on the super-freeze setting. Quick-frozen foods have smaller ice crystals, which means they thaw without losing moisture and nutrients.

Freeze soups, stews and sauces in portions, so you can defrost the right amount when needed. Leftover wine, stock and chopped herbs (immersed in a little water) can be frozen in ice cube trays, then transferred to a zip-lock freezer bag. Make the most of precious freezer space by freezing stews and sauces flat in thick freezer bags. Plastic containers with tight-fitting lids are useful, too; try empty, well-washed ice cream tubs, margarine containers and yogurt pots.

'Tray-freezing' is an ideal way to freeze fruit and vegetables as well as vegetarian sausage rolls, burgers, pastries, patties and pies to keep them separate and prevent them sticking together during freezing. When frozen, transfer them to an appropriate bag or container. Wrap individual items in clingfilm first to keep them separate. If freezing your own food, make sure it has cooled down, as warm foods raise the internal temperature of the freezer and could affect other foods. It's a good idea to write the name, portion size and date of freezing – or be super-efficient and keep a record of the contents of your freezer so things don't get forgotten about.

Defrost foods at room temperature (about 18°C/65°F) or in the fridge if time allows. You can also defrost foods in the microwave or oven, but this may affect their texture. Last but not least, avoid re-freezing previously defrosted food.

GROW-YOUR-OWN

I'm a relative newbie to the world of vegetable growing. Over the years I've had some success growing veg in my small patio garden, in pots, grow-bags and beds, and have had a herb garden for as long as I can remember, but I've recently joined forces with a few friends on an allotment and we've been rewarded with a bounteous supply of fresh produce. An increasing number of people have got hooked on growing their own fresh fruit and vegetables, but if it's not for you then the next best thing is a local box delivery scheme or farmers' market.

The grow-your-own tips in *Veggienomics* arm you with the basics and focus on the fresh produce that I've grown myself. Unfortunately, there was not enough space to go into much detail (which is why I haven't gone into seed varieties) but hopefully I've given you enough to inspire you to try growing your own veg, as well as highlighting any planting idiosyncrasies. If you do have a glut of vegetables, they freeze well, but it's best to blanch and refresh them first as then they tend to keep better. Alternatively, freeze them uncooked, but do cook them soon after defrosting.

If you intend to preserve your homegrown produce (or indeed foraging finds), by turning it into jams, jellies, chutneys or pickles, you must sterilize the jars you intend to use first to avoid contamination and spoilage. This is easy to do, but it's vital to pay careful attention to hygiene. Wash new or reused jars (removing any labels first) well in hot soapy water, then rinse and place them on a baking tray in a cold oven. Turn the oven to 180°C/350°F/Gas 4 and, once it has reached this temperature, leave the jars in the oven for 10 minutes. Use new lids, rather than renewing the old ones, and sterilize them before potting by boiling them in a pan of water for 10 minutes. Carefully remove with tongs and leave to dry. Pot your preserves when they are still warm and cover with the lids. You may have to tighten the lids as they cool.

FOOD FOR FREE

Foraging is immensely pleasurable – there is little more rewarding than finding edible delights that are absolutely free. It's a great way to get in touch with the seasons, as well as discovering that many of the so-called 'weeds' you've walked past for years are actually edible plants – and taste good, too.

Many of the recipes in this book contain wild foods: from coastal vegetables, flowers and nuts to herbs, mushrooms and greens, yet my selection just scratches the surface of what can be found. This taste of foraging will hopefully inspire you to go out and gather, if you haven't already done so. Be respectful of nature when foraging, do not uproot plants or pick greedily, and also make sure the plants you are picking aren't a protected species. A good foraging book is a must for identifying wild foods, and is imperative when looking for fungi. It will help you discover the edible wonders of the countryside and coastline – and cities can be surprisingly fruitful, too.

Basics and Accompaniments

The purpose of this eclectic collection of recipes is two-fold—
some of the recipes form the foundation of dishes contained
within the main chapters, while others are accompaniments
that will embellish and enhance meals. For instance, no kitchen
should be without a good, staple vegetable stock recipe.
It is the base for many recipes in the book and can be stored
portioned in the freezer. At the other end of the scale is the
Korean condiment, kimchi, a potent pickle that's great with
Asian dishes, pies or cheese platters. There are also useful
recipes for thick plain yogurt, pastry, spice mix and salsas,
and don't miss trying the Quick Preserved Lemons.

This makes a basic, light savoury pastry, which is ideal for lining and topping flans and pies. For a richer pastry, you could add an egg to the dough and reduce the milk to 1–2 tablespoons. For a sweet pastry, stir in 60g/2¼oz/scant ⅓ cup caster sugar at the end of Step 1. The pastry is made by hand, but you can use a food processor instead.

Shortcrust Pastry

Makes: enough to line a 28cm/11¼in flan tin   *Preparation time:* 10 minutes, plus 30 minutes chilling

225g/8oz/heaped 1¾ cups plain flour
a pinch of salt

115g/4oz cold butter, cut into small, even-sized pieces
about 60ml/2fl oz/¼ cup milk

1. Sift the flour and salt into a bowl, stir until combined, then add the butter. Lightly rub in the butter with your fingertips until the mixture resembles fine breadcrumbs.

2. Gradually stir in the milk until the crumbs start to come together, then knead briefly into a smooth ball of dough. Wrap in cling film, press into a disc and chill for 30 minutes in the fridge until ready to use.

Uncooked pastry can be frozen for up to 3 months. Put the disc or sheet of pastry in a freezer-proof bag and freeze in a greaseproof paper-lined baking tray before transferring to a zip-lock freezer bag.

This recipe is just a general guide, as you can make stock from any vegetables you have to hand. Root vegetables make a good starting point, but avoid using too much of one type as it will dominate the flavour. Salt isn't added to the stock, as you will probably be using it in another recipe, and this will enable you to control how salty the final dish is.

Vegetable Stock

Makes: 1.75l/60fl oz/6⅔ cups   **Preparation time:** 10 minutes
Cooking time: 1 hour 10 minutes

2 tbsp olive oil
2 onions, chopped
2 leeks, chopped
3 celery sticks, chopped
3 carrots, chopped
1 turnip, chopped

3 garlic cloves, peeled and crushed
6 parsley sprigs
2 bay leaves
1 small handful of thyme sprigs
½ tsp peppercorns

1. Heat the oil in a large, heavy-based saucepan over a medium heat. Add the vegetables and cook for 10 minutes, part-covered and stirring occasionally, until softened. Stir in the garlic, parsley, bay leaves, thyme and peppercorns.

2. Pour in 1.75l/60fl oz/6⅔ cups water and bring to the boil, then turn the heat down and simmer over a low heat for 1 hour. Strain the stock, discard the solids and leave it to cool. Keep in the fridge for up to 1 week or freeze in portions.

This forms the base of Asian soups, curries and stir-fries.

Asian Stock

Makes: *about 1.2l/40fl oz/4¾ cups* **Preparation time:** *10 minutes, plus making the stock and 1 hour infusing* **Cooking time:** *10 minutes*

⅔ **recipe quantity Vegetable Stock (opposite)**
2 lemongrass stalks, bruised
1 long cinnamon stick
2 star anise

6 cardamom pods, split
6 cloves
5cm/2in piece of root ginger, sliced
    into thin rounds

1. Put the stock, lemongrass, cinnamon, star anise, cardamom, cloves and ginger in a large saucepan and bring to the boil, then turn the heat down and simmer, part-covered, for 10 minutes. Remove from the heat and leave to infuse for 1 hour. Use as instructed, or cool and then chill or freeze.

This aromatic blend of spices works well in both coconut-based and tomato-based Indian curries. Keep any unused spice mix in a jar with a lid and store in a cool, dark place.

Curry Spice Mix

Makes: *enough for 4 curries* **Preparation time:** *10 minutes*
Cooking time: *2 minutes*

2 tbsp coriander seeds
2 tsp cumin seeds
2 tbsp fenugreek seeds
12 cardamom pods, seeds removed

1 tsp cloves
4 dried red chillies
2 tsp turmeric
1 tsp ground cinnamon

1. Put the coriander, cumin, fenugreek and cardamom seeds in a large, dry frying pan. Add the cloves and chillies and toast for 1–2 minutes over a medium-low heat, shaking the pan occasionally, until the spices smell aromatic and slightly toasted.

2. Tip the spices into a mortar and, using a pestle, grind to a powder, or use a spice grinder. Stir in the turmeric and cinnamon and store in a lidded jar in a cool, dark place.

Rich, creamy, delicious and much cheaper than shop-bought, you don't need a special yogurt maker to make this, but a kitchen thermometer is recommended. It's also important to be scrupulous about hygiene and make sure all your equipment is clean to avoid contamination. Depending on the time of year, you may need to consider how to keep the yogurt warm while it cultures. It's obviously much easier when it's warm, but in the winter months it helps if you have an airing cupboard or thermos flask. For a lighter, low-fat yogurt, use semi-skimmed milk instead and leave out the double cream.

Wholemilk Yogurt

Makes: *about 1l/35fl oz/4 cups*   **Preparation time:** *55 minutes, plus 8 hours cooling and fermenting*   **Cooking time:** *25 minutes*

1l/35fl oz/4 cups full-fat milk,
   preferably organic

4 tbsp double cream
4 tbsp natural live or bio yogurt

1. Slowly warm the milk in a large, heavy-based saucepan over a medium-low heat, stirring occasionally, until bubbles start to appear on the surface; it should read 85°C/185°F on the thermometer. Once the milk has reached this heat, keep it there for about 20 minutes, or until it has reduced by a quarter, stirring occasionally. You may need to turn the heat down to low during this time.

2. Turn the heat off, remove any skin that has formed on the surface of the milk and stir in the cream. Leave the mixture to cool to 43°C/110°F, stirring occasionally. This usually takes around 40–45 minutes.

3. Put the live yogurt in a 1l/35fl oz/4 cup sterilized Mason jar (see page 11) and pour in a quarter of the milk mixture. Stir until combined, then add the remaining milk mixture and stir again. Fasten the lid and wrap in cling film, a towel, then a black plastic bag to keep the warmth in. Leave in a warm place, ideally around 40°C/104°F, for 5–8 hours or until thickened. Stir well and chill in the fridge until ready to eat. It will keep for up to 1 week.

To make the most delicious cream cheese, stir 1 tsp sea salt into the yogurt, then drain in a muslin-lined sieve overnight in the fridge to remove the whey.

If you like the idea of making cheese, then a simple, drained curd cheese is the perfect starting point – it's easy and requires no specialist equipment or ingredients. Paneer is a delicate, milky, soft cheese, often used in Indian dishes. It can also be cut into cubes or crumbled over salads, pizzas or tagines, or used as part of a filling in savoury filo or puff pastry parcels. Shop-bought paneer tends to have a firmer texture and is good stir-fried until golden.

Homemade Paneer

Makes: 450g/1lb *Preparation time:* 10 minutes, plus 1 hour draining and 1 hour pressing *Cooking time:* 10 minutes

1l/35fl oz/4 cups full-fat milk
2–3 tbsp lemon juice
1 tsp fine sea salt

1. Line a colander or sieve with a double layer of clean muslin or cheesecloth. Pour the milk into a pan and bring to the boil, then turn the heat down to low. Add 2 tablespoons of the lemon juice and stir until the milk separates into curds and whey. If the milk takes longer than a minute to curdle, add the remaining lemon juice to help get it going.

2. Remove the pan from the heat and pour the mixture into the lined colander. Rinse the curds briefly under cold running water to remove any sour residue from the lemon and stir in the salt. Draw up the corners of the muslin, twist to make a bundle and squeeze gently to remove as much liquid as possible. Press into a round disc and leave the curds to drain in the colander over a large mixing bowl for 1 hour.

3. When fully drained, put the muslin-covered curd parcel on a plate and press under a heavy weight. Put it in the fridge and leave for 1 hour. Once the cheese is pressed, you can leave it whole or cut into cubes and store in a container covered with lightly salted water for up to 4 days.

The lemon juice is added to encourage the heated milk to form curds, but the same quantity of buttermilk or thick natural yogurt will do the same job.

Roasting intensifies the flavour of nuts (and seeds) as well as giving them more of a crunch. You get a more even roasting and colour if this is done in the oven, rather than in a dry frying pan, but if you only need a small quantity, then pan-toasting makes more sense. If I happen to be using the oven, I make the most of the space and heat by toasting the nuts in bulk; they'll keep for a week or so in an airtight container.

Roasted Nuts (and Seeds)

Makes: 2–4 handfuls   **Preparation time:** 5 minutes
Cooking time: 15 minutes

2–4 handfuls of shelled nuts (or seeds) of choice

1. Preheat the oven to 180°C/350°F/Gas 4. Line one or two baking sheets with baking parchment and put the nuts (or seeds) in an even layer on top. Place the sheet(s) in the bottom half of the oven and roast for 12–15 minutes (6–10 minutes for seeds), turning twice, until toasted and evenly browned. Keep an eye on them as they can burn easily. Alternatively, for small quantities of nuts (or seeds), put them in a dry, heavy-based frying pan in an even layer. Toast over a medium-low heat for 8–10 minutes (5–7 minutes for seeds; 2–3 minutes for small seeds such as sesame), regularly shaking the pan, until toasted and evenly browned. Leave to cool and store in an airtight container.

If you regularly eat nuts and seeds it pays to buy them in large quantities. If packed in a plastic bag, transfer them after opening to an airtight container and store in a cool place – even the fridge or freezer – to keep them fresh. You don't have to defrost nuts and seeds before use.

A spoonful of this lightly spiced fresh mango chutney perks up curries, but is equally good served with cheese and crusty bread. Peaches, nectarines or pineapple would work as well as the mango, so feel free to adapt depending on what fruit you have available.

Mango Chutney

Makes: *300ml/10½fl oz/scant 1¼ cups*   **Preparation time:** *10 minutes*
Cooking time: *30 minutes*

1 tbsp coriander seeds
1 tbsp sunflower oil
1 small onion, finely chopped
1 green chilli, finely chopped (no need
   to deseed)
4cm/1½in piece of root ginger, peeled and
   very finely chopped

8 cloves
1 large ripe mango, stoned and diced
4 tbsp white wine vinegar
4 tbsp soft light brown sugar
sea salt and freshly ground black pepper

1. Toast the coriander seeds in a large, dry frying pan over a medium-low heat for 2 minutes, or until aromatic. Lightly crush with a pestle and mortar or the end of a rolling pin. Leave to one side.

2. Heat the oil in the frying pan over a medium heat. Add the onion and fry for 7 minutes until tender but not coloured. Stir in the chilli, ginger and cloves, then add the mango, 4 tablespoons water, the vinegar and sugar, and stir well and simmer for 20 minutes until reduced and thickened. Season with salt and pepper, then taste, adding more sugar or vinegar as needed.

3. Spoon the chutney into sterilized jars (see page 11) or into a bowl and leave to cool. The chutney can be eaten straightaway but its flavour will develop with time. It will keep for up to 2 weeks in the fridge.

This popular spicy Korean pickle is the classic accompaniment to the rice dish Bibimbap (see page 75), but a spoonful will lift any Asian rice or noodle dish. The Asian radish, daikon or mooli is traditional but I find turnip is just as good, easier to find and more economical to buy.

Kimchi

Makes: *750ml/26fl oz/3 cups*   **Preparation time:** *2½ days*

165g/5¾oz/¾ cup salt, plus extra for sprinkling
750g/1lb 10oz Chinese leaves, halved
    crossways and cut into 4 wedges, tough
    stalk removed
375g/13oz turnip, peeled and coarsely grated
3 tbsp dark soy sauce
2 tsp mild Korean red pepper powder, Aleppo
    chilli flakes or mild cayenne pepper

2 tbsp gochujang (Korean hot chilli paste)
    or other hot chilli paste
2.5cm/1in piece of root ginger, grated
    (no need to peel)
2 garlic cloves, finely chopped
1 tbsp caster sugar
1 tbsp sesame seeds, toasted
4 spring onions, sliced
1 tsp sesame oil

1. Dissolve the salt in 2l/70fl oz/8 cups water in a large bowl. Sprinkle extra salt between the leaves of the cabbage. Put the cabbage in the salty water and put a weighted plate on top to keep it submerged. Leave to soak for 3 hours, or until the cabbage leaves are pliable and do not break when bent.

2. Using a slotted spoon, scoop the cabbage out of the water into a large colander and add the turnip to the salted water. Rinse the cabbage well under cold running water (this is important or it will be too salty) and leave to drain for 30 minutes while the turnip is soaking.

3. Mix together the soy sauce, red pepper powder, chilli paste, ginger, garlic, sugar, sesame seeds, spring onions and sesame oil in a large bowl.

4. Squeeze the cabbage to remove any excess water and pat dry with a clean tea towel. Slice the cabbage crossways into large, bite-sized pieces and add to the bowl with the flavourings. Drain and rinse the turnip well, drain again and pat dry in a clean tea towel. Add to the bowl with the cabbage and stir until everything is combined. Spoon the kimchi into a sterilized Mason jar (see page 11) and press down with the back of the spoon. Put the lid on and leave in a cool, dark place for 2 days before eating to allow the flavours to develop, then transfer to a fridge. It will keep for several months in the fridge.

A piquant, fruity salsa that is good as a topping for bruschetta, served with roasted or barbecued vegetables, or as an accompaniment to the Goats' Cheese Pancakes (see page 138).

Pomegranate Salsa

Serves: 4   *Preparation time:* 15 minutes   *Cooking time:* 35 minutes

1 tbsp olive oil
1 onion, finely chopped
5 garlic cloves, finely chopped
150ml/5fl oz/scant ⅔ cup white wine vinegar
150ml/5fl oz/scant ⅔ cup fresh orange juice
40g/1½oz/scant ¼ cup soft light brown sugar

seeds from 1 small pomegranate
2 handfuls of pistachio nuts, toasted
  (see page 18) and chopped
25g/1oz mint leaves, roughly chopped
sea salt and freshly ground black pepper

1. Heat the oil in a saucepan over a medium heat. Add the onion and fry for 10 minutes until softened and starting to colour, then add the garlic and cook for another 2 minutes. Stir in the vinegar, orange juice and sugar, then turn the heat down to low and simmer for 25 minutes, stirring occasionally, until the liquid has reduced and become syrupy. Season well with salt and pepper.

2. Transfer to a bowl and leave to cool slightly before stirring in the pomegranate seeds, pistachios and mint.

Middle Eastern grocers are great places to buy large bunches of fresh herbs at a fraction of the cost of those sold in supermarkets. To keep them fresh for a week or more, wrap the root end in a damp piece of kitchen paper, secure with an elastic band and store in a plastic bag. Alternatively remove the leaves from the stems and freeze them separately in plastic containers for future use.

This salsa crops up a fair bit in this book — I find it a great and easy way to add flavour, texture and interest to all sorts of dishes.

Tomato and Chilli Salsa

Serves: 4   **Preparation time:** 15 minutes

4 large vine-ripened tomatoes, deseeded
   and diced
¼ red onion, diced
2 heaped tbsp bottled jalapeño chillies,
   drained and chopped

2 handfuls of coriander, chopped
juice of 1 lime
2 tbsp extra virgin olive oil
sea salt and freshly ground black pepper

1. Mix together all the ingredients for the salsa in a bowl. Season with salt and pepper and serve at room temperature.

This garlicky sweet potato and coconut milk mash is served with the Eggs with Lemongrass Cream (see page 125), but could be served topped with strips of omelette, marinated fried tofu or roasted vegetables.

Asian-Style Mash

Serves: 4   **Preparation time:** 15 minutes   **Cooking time:** 15 minutes

425g/15oz sweet potatoes, peeled and cut into
   large pieces
425g/15oz white potatoes, peeled and cut into
   large pieces
3 spring onions, chopped

4 garlic cloves
100ml/3½fl oz/scant ½ cup coconut milk
juice of ½ lime
1 medium red chilli, deseeded and
   finely chopped

1. Put both types of potato, the spring onions (reserving a third of the green parts to serve) and garlic in a large saucepan, cover with just-boiled water from a kettle and return to the boil. Turn the heat down slightly and simmer, part-covered, for 10–15 minutes, or until tender. Drain and return the potatoes to the pan and let them dry briefly in the heat of the pan.

2. Add the coconut milk, lime juice and chilli to the pan, season with salt and pepper and mash until smooth. Serve straightaway.

A sprinkling of crisp, golden onions and ginger adds the finishing touch to Asian stir-fries, curries and salads. In fact, why be restricted to Asian food? I'd be tempted to add a spoonful to whatever you feel would benefit. It makes sense to cook up a large batch and then store any leftovers in an airtight container, lined with kitchen paper, in the fridge.

Crispy Onions and Ginger

Serves: 6–8 **Preparation time:** *10 minutes* **Cooking time:** *11 minutes*

250ml/9fl oz/1 cup sunflower oil
2 onions, halved and thinly sliced into
   half-moons

10cm/4in piece of root ginger, peeled and cut
   into thin julienne strips

1. Heat the oil in a deep, heavy-based pan over a medium heat. Add the onions and fry for 6–8 minutes or until golden and crisp. They will crisp up further as they cool. Remove with a slotted spoon and drain on a double layer of kitchen paper.

2. Add the ginger to the pan and fry for 3 minutes, or until golden and crisp. Drain the ginger and combine with the cooked onions. Leave to cool before using.

Shop-bought preserved lemons can be fiendishly expensive, so not wishing to splash out or be left with a half-used jar in the fridge, I was eager to try a friend's speedy alternative – and the results were so good. Usually preserved lemons take months to preserve, but these take a matter of minutes and you still get that wonderful salty, lemony tang, which characterizes the traditionally made alternative.

Quick Preserved Lemons

Makes: *200ml/7fl oz/scant 1 cup* **Preparation time:** *10 minutes, plus cooling* **Cooking time:** *15 minutes*

6 unwaxed lemons
1½ tsp sea salt

1. Use a vegetable peeler to pare off the skin of each lemon, cut in half, then squeeze the juice and remove any pips. Put the lemon skin and juice and salt into a non-reactive, small saucepan and slowly bring to boiling heat. Turn the heat down and simmer for 10–12 minutes until the lemon skins are tender and the juice has reduced.

2. Transfer to a bowl and leave to cool. Use the preserved lemons straight away or spoon into an airtight container and store in the fridge for up to 2 weeks.

Elderflowers have a relatively short life so it makes sense to grab the opportunity to use them in cooking. A spoonful of this light and delicately fragrant syrup adds a touch of sweetness to marinades or dressings, or it can be used to flavour the poaching liquid for pears (see page 132) or other orchard fruit. Diluted with sparkling water or soda, it makes a refreshing, summery drink.

Elderflower Syrup

Makes: about 1l/35fl oz/4 cups   *Preparation time:* 15 minutes, plus 3 days infusing   *Cooking time:* 10 minutes

23 large elderflower heads
juice and finely grated zest of 5 lemons
1kg/2lb 4oz/4¾ cups caster sugar

1. Shake the elderflower heads to remove any dirt or bugs, then strip the flowers off the stalks and put them in a large heatproof bowl with the lemon juice and zest.

2. Meanwhile, bring 1l/35fl oz/4 cups water to the boil in a pan. Stir in the sugar until dissolved, then boil for 6–8 minutes until you have a light syrup.

3. Pour the syrup over the flower mixture, stir well, then cover and leave to infuse for 3 days. Strain the flowers through a sieve and pour the syrup into sterilized bottles (see page 11). The syrup will keep in the fridge for up to 1 month.

Chapter 1
Tin of Beans (and Other Pulses)

You can't get a more humble food than a bean, yet the recipes here show that it's perfectly possible to create truly delicious meals with something so simple and unassuming: there's spicy Black Bean Tostados with tangy Lime Cream, a filling Lentil, Preserved Lemon and Date Tagine and a quick-to-make Edamame and Wasabi Hummus, and that's just a taster ... All recipes give instructions for using tinned or dried beans, allowing you to make the most of what you have to hand.

Small bags of Chinese fermented black beans can be bought from Asian grocers, and any leftovers will keep for months in an airtight container in the fridge. They're inexpensive, and pack a powerful punch. You could add cooked noodles or rice to this soup for a more substantial meal.

Oriental Black Bean and Mushroom Broth

Serves: 4   **Preparation time:** *15 minutes, plus making the stock and 30 minutes soaking and infusing*   **Cooking time:** *10 minutes*

1l/35fl oz/4 cups Vegetable Stock
   (see page 14)
2 star anise
2.5cm/1in piece of root ginger, peeled
   and cut into rounds
2 tbsp soy sauce
2 garlic cloves, halved
4 tbsp Chinese fermented black beans
200g/7oz shiitake or chestnut mushrooms,
   thinly sliced

1 long red chilli, deseeded and thinly sliced
2 large handfuls of baby spinach leaves
100g/3½oz sugar snap peas, sliced diagonally

TO SERVE
2 tsp toasted sesame oil
2 eggs, lightly beaten
1 small handful of bean sprouts
2 spring onions, thinly sliced on the diagonal
1 tbsp chopped roasted unsalted peanuts

1. Put the stock in a large saucepan and add the star anise, ginger, soy sauce and garlic. Bring to the boil over a medium heat, then turn the heat off and leave to infuse for 30 minutes, covered with a lid. Remove the flavourings with a slotted spoon.

2. Meanwhile, put the black beans in a small bowl, cover with 200ml/7fl oz/scant 1 cup just-boiled water and leave to soak for 30 minutes. Strain the beans, reserving the soaking liquor for another recipe (see below), and add the beans to the flavoured stock with the mushrooms and half the chilli. Bring to the boil, then turn the heat down and simmer for 1 minute. Add the spinach and sugar snaps, stir and simmer for another 3 minutes until tender.

3. While the broth is simmering, make an omelette. Heat the sesame oil in a large, non-stick frying pan, pour in the eggs, swirl the pan so they cover the base and cook for 2 minutes until set. Roll up the omelette with a spatula, tip onto a board and cut crossways into thin strips. Ladle the soup into four wide bowls and top with the omelette strips, bean sprouts, remaining chilli, spring onions and peanuts.

Freeze the soaking liquor from the fermented black beans in an ice cube tray. Transfer the cubes to a zip-lock bag and return to the freezer. Use as a flavoursome stock.

Chinese black beans are also used in Chinese Black Bean and Mozzarella Salad (page 151).

To **sprout your own beans or seeds**, soak them in tepid water for 12 hours, then drain and put in a clean jam jar. Cover with muslin and secure with a rubber band, then stand the jar in a light, draught-free place. Rinse twice a day under cold water (don't remove the muslin), then drain. The sprouts are ready when they're 2.5cm/1in long. Store in an airtight container in the fridge for up to 1 week.

Dandelions

grow profusely and you can forage for them at any time of the year, although I always pick the *young spring leaves* because they are less bitter. Choose a spot where they grow that is free from any kind of contamination – traffic and dogs, for example – and pick the leaves from the base of the plant. Trim the leaves and wash them well before use.

In southern Italy's Puglia region, this fava bean (dried broad bean) purée is a winter staple and a popular antipasto. Made from basic seasonal ingredients, it is pure comfort food when spread over crusty bread and doubles up as a satisfying side dish. The Pugliese serve it with bitter greens such as wild chicory, but you could use spinach, rocket, sea beet, nettles or broccoli rabe. I've gone for a mixture of young dandelion and beet leaves.

Fava Bean Purée

Serves: *4–6* **Preparation time:** *15 minutes, plus overnight soaking*
Cooking time: *1 hour*

200g/7oz/1 cup split fava beans, soaked
  overnight, drained and rinsed
300g/10½oz white potatoes, peeled and
  thickly sliced
75g/2½oz young dandelion leaves,
  roughly chopped
100g/3½oz beet greens, tough stalks
  removed, leaves shredded
juice of ½ lemon

5 tbsp extra virgin olive oil, plus extra
  for drizzling
sea salt and freshly ground black pepper

TO SERVE
4–8 thick slices of country-style bread
2 garlic cloves, halved
4 vines of ripened cherry tomatoes

1. Tip the fava beans into a large saucepan, cover with plenty of cold water and bring to the boil, then turn the heat down slightly and boil gently for 40 minutes until tender. Drain the beans and return to the pan with the potatoes. Cover with water and bring to the boil, then turn the heat down and simmer for 20 minutes, or until the potatoes and beans are soft.

2. Meanwhile, put the dandelion leaves and beet leaves in a pan with a splash of water. Add a good pinch of salt to the pan and cook, covered, over a low heat for 3 minutes until softened. Stir the leaves occasionally so they cook evenly. Drain away any bitter juices, add another splash of water and cook, uncovered, for another 2 minutes, or until the leaves are very tender and the water has evaporated. Drain off any excess water and leave to one side.

3. Drain the fava beans and potatoes, reserving the cooking water, and return the beans and potatoes to the pan. Season well with salt and pepper and mash with a potato masher, adding the lemon juice and some of the reserved cooking water to make a thick, smooth, fluffy purée. Beat in the olive oil until combined. Transfer to a bowl and drizzle with oil. Toast the bread and rub one side of each slice with the cut side of a garlic clove. Serve the bean purée warm topped with the greens and extra oil with the garlic toasts and tomatoes.

Any leftover purée can be mixed with a beaten egg and formed into patties. Dust them in flour and fry in sunflower oil until crisp and golden.

A bag of frozen edamame (soya) beans makes a useful freezer standby for adding to stir-fries, soups or salads, or puréed – as here – to make a dip. Instead of adding wasabi, you can alter the flavourings to make a Moroccan-style hummus by adding extra tahini, ground coriander and cumin, and a little harissa. In keeping with the Asian feel, the hummus comes with wonton crisps.

Edamame and Wasabi Hummus

Serves: 4–6   *Preparation time:* 10 minutes, plus cooling
Cooking time: 5 minutes

150g/5½oz/1 heaped cup frozen edamame (soya) beans
2 tsp wasabi paste
juice of 1½ unwaxed limes
2 tbsp light olive oil, plus extra for frying
1 tbsp light tahini

1 tbsp snipped chives
1 tbsp sesame seeds, toasted (see page 18), plus extra for sprinkling
sea salt and freshly ground black pepper
8–12 wonton wrappers for frying, to serve

1. Cook the edamame in a pan of boiling salted water for 5 minutes until tender, then leave to cool in their cooking water. Drain the beans, reserving 4–6 tablespoons of the cooking water.

2. Put the cooled beans, reserving a handful, in a blender with the wasabi, lime juice, olive oil, tahini and reserved water, and blend to a coarse paste. Spoon the hummus into a serving bowl and season with salt and pepper. Serve at room temperature topped with the reserved beans, chives and sesame seeds.

3. To make the wonton crisps, pour in enough oil to coat the base of a large frying pan and heat over a medium heat. Fry the wontons in batches for 1–2 minutes each side until crisp and golden. Drain on kitchen paper and, while still warm, season with salt and pepper and scatter sesame seeds on top.

Use the hummus as the filling for Wonton Ravioli (see page 59).

Finely grate the zest of the limes before you extract the juice, and store in a small airtight container in the freezer for up to 3 months. Use straight from frozen whenever a recipe calls for lime zest. Orange and lemon zest can be frozen and used in the same way, too.

If you haven't tried squash seeds, you'll find they're too good to throw away, and are reminiscent of pumpkin seeds. Roast them to scatter over this North African-inspired salad, or eat as a snack sprinkled with soy sauce.

Puy Lentil, Squash and Crispy Chickpea Salad

Serves: *4* **Preparation time:** *20 minutes* **Cooking time:** *50 minutes*

6 tbsp extra virgin olive oil
3 heaped tsp harissa
1 small butternut squash, peeled, seeds reserved, cut into bite-sized cubes
2 red onions, each cut into 8 wedges
125g/4½oz/1 cup drained tinned chickpeas or cooked dried chickpeas (see pages 8–9)
250g/9oz/heaped 1¼ cups dried Puy lentils

½ tsp cumin seeds
1 handful of parsley leaves, chopped
1 handful of coriander leaves chopped
juice and finely grated zest of 1 large unwaxed lemon
125g/4½oz rindless goats' cheese, crumbled
sea salt and freshly ground black pepper

1. Preheat the oven to 200°C/400°F/Gas 6. Mix together 2 tablespoons of the oil and half the harissa in a large bowl. Season with salt and pepper and add the squash and onions, turn to coat them in the harissa oil, then tip into a large roasting tin and spread out in a single layer.

2. Wash the squash seeds, then add to the bowl with the chickpeas. Pour in 1 tablespoon of the oil and the remaining harissa, turn until coated and tip out into a second large roasting tin. Spread them out in a single layer. Put both trays in the oven and roast for 35–40 minutes, turning once, until the squash and onions are tender and slightly golden and the chickpeas and seeds are crisp.

3. Meanwhile, put the lentils in a saucepan, cover with plenty of cold water and bring to the boil. Turn the heat down to medium-low, part-cover with a lid and simmer for 25 minutes until tender. Drain and tip into a serving bowl. Add the roasted squash, onions, cumin and herbs to the lentils. Mix together the remaining oil and lemon juice and zest, season with salt and pepper and pour it over the salad. Toss, then sprinkle with the goats' cheese, chickpeas and 2 tablespoons of the squash seeds. The remaining squash seeds can be eaten separately as a snack.

Save time by cooking dried chickpeas in bulk (see pages 8–9), and store unused chickpeas in the fridge for up to 3 days or in the freezer for up to 3 months. There's no need to defrost them for soups, stews or sauces.

Many of my recipes come about through a need to use up a motley collection of ingredients in the fridge or cupboard, and this is one of them. A packet of dried green lentils and some ready-to-eat dried dates had been lurking in the cupboard and were crying out to be used. I also picked up a recipe for super-quick preserved lemons from a friend and was eager to put it to use. Jars of preserved lemons are prohibitively expensive and this version is a fantastically easy and economical alternative.

Lentil, Preserved Lemon and Date Tagine

Serves: *4–6*   **Preparation time:** *20 minutes, plus making the stock*
Cooking time: *35 minutes*

1 tbsp olive oil
1 large onion, chopped
3 carrots, halved lengthways and cut into
    bite-sized chunks
2 turnips, peeled and cut into bite-sized chunks
3 garlic cloves, chopped
2 tsp coriander seeds
2 cinnamon sticks
2 tsp ground cumin
1 tsp turmeric powder
½ tsp ground ginger

½ tsp dried chilli flakes
140g/5oz/¾ cup dried green lentils
875ml/30fl oz/3½ cups hot Vegetable Stock
    (see page 14)
115g/4oz/⅔ cup ready-to-eat pitted dried
    dates, halved
1 tbsp Quick Preserved Lemons (see page 24)
sea salt and freshly ground black pepper
1 handful of coriander leaves, chopped, and
    couscous, to serve

1. Heat the olive oil in a large casserole over a medium heat. Add the onion and cook for 5 minutes until softened. Turn the heat down slightly and add the carrots, turnips, garlic and coriander seeds and cook, part-covered, for another 5 minutes, stirring regularly, until the carrots have softened slightly.

2. Stir in the cinnamon sticks, ground spices and chilli flakes, then add the lentils. Pour in the stock, stir well and bring to the boil. Turn the heat down to low, part-cover the pan with a lid and simmer for 15 minutes until the lentils are almost tender.

3. Stir in the dates and the preserved lemons and cook, covered, for 10 minutes, or until the lentils are tender. Add a splash more stock or water, if the tagine needs it. Season with salt and pepper, scatter the coriander over and serve in bowls with couscous by the side.

Why buy a tin of refried beans when you can make your own for less, and they taste a whole lot better? Snack packs of four small avocados tend to be more economical than individual ones, and are just the right size for salads.

Black Bean Tostados with Lime Cream

Serves: 4   *Preparation time:* 15 minutes   *Cooking time:* 10 minutes

300g/10½oz/2½ cups drained tinned black
   beans, liquid reserved, or cooked dried
   black beans (see pages 8–9), reserving
   4 tablespoons of the cooking water
½ red onion, halved
1 large garlic clove
juice of ½ lime
2 tbsp olive oil
2 tsp chipotle chilli paste
1 tsp ground cumin
1 tsp ground coriander

4 soft corn tortillas
½ Romaine lettuce, shredded
2 small avocados, pitted, peeled and sliced
125g/4½oz/1 cup feta cheese, crumbled
sea salt and freshly ground black pepper
1 recipe quantity Tomato and Chilli Salsa
   (see page 22), to serve

LIME CREAM
100ml/3½fl oz/scant ½ cup crème fraîche
finely grated zest of ½ unwaxed lime

1. Mix together the ingredients for the lime cream in a bowl, cover and leave in the fridge until needed.

2. Put half the black beans and the onion, garlic, lime juice and 4 tablespoons of the drained liquid from the beans in a blender. Pulse briefly to a coarse purée, then tip into a medium, non-stick frying pan with 1 tablespoon of the oil, the remaining beans, chipotle chilli paste, cumin and coriander. Season with salt and pepper, stir and cook over a medium-low heat for 5 minutes until heated through.

3. Meanwhile, heat the remaining oil in a separate frying pan and cook the tortillas, one at a time, for 1 minute on each side until heated through and golden in places. Put a tortilla on each serving plate and top with the lettuce, refried beans, avocados and feta. Serve with the salsa and lime cream.

A tip for cooking dried beans is to add a 13cm/5in strip of kombu (dried kelp used in Japanese cooking) to the cooking liquid. This helps soften the outer skin and gives a creamier, softer texture. The kombu works by breaking down the starchy carbohydrates in the beans.

If you have memories of soggy, mealy butter beans served up for school dinner, ditch that thought now and try them in this light, summery stew. One of my favourite spices is hot smoked paprika – it not only satisfies my love of chilli-heat, but its wonderful smokiness brings a dish together.

Spanish-Style White Beans

Serves: 4   **Preparation time:** 15 minutes, plus making the stock
Cooking time: 45 minutes

3 tbsp extra virgin olive oil
1 large onion, chopped
3 large garlic cloves, thinly sliced
1 large red pepper, deseeded and chopped
2 courgettes, thickly sliced, then each
   slice quartered
170ml/5½fl oz/⅔ cup dry white wine or extra
   vegetable stock (see below)
500ml/17fl oz/2 cups passata
150ml/5fl oz/scant ⅔ cup Vegetable Stock
   (see page 14)

1 tsp sugar
300g/10½oz/2½ cups drained tinned butter
   beans, or cooked dried butter beans
   (see pages 8–9)
2 bay leaves
1 tbsp thyme leaves or 2 tsp dried thyme
1–2 tsp hot smoked paprika
3 handfuls of curly kale or cavalo nero,
   tough stalks removed, leaves shredded
sea salt and freshly ground black pepper
soured cream and crusty bread, to serve

1. Heat the olive oil in a large casserole over a medium heat. Add the onion and fry for 6 minutes until softened. Add the garlic, red pepper and courgettes and cook for another 5 minutes until just tender.

2. Pour in the wine and bring to the boil. Cook until reduced by half, then add the passata and vegetable stock and bring to the boil. Turn the heat down to low, add the sugar, butter beans, bay leaves, thyme and paprika, and simmer, part-covered, for 30 minutes until the sauce has reduced and thickened.

3. Stir in the kale, season with salt and pepper and cook for another 3 minutes until wilted. Serve with crusty bread, and topped with a spoonful of soured cream.

Save time and freezer space by freezing stews, soups, sauces and curries flat. Once cool, transfer to a zip-lock bag and place on a baking sheet in the freezer. To defrost, hold under a hot tap for a few seconds, then unzip the bag and tip the contents into a pan to reheat.

In a small garden, grow **courgettes** in pots. The seeds should be sown indoors in mid-spring, and the young plants planted out when there is no risk of frost. Female stems have a small bulge behind the flower that will turn into a courgette; males just produce flowers. Don't waste the flowers – harvest them early in the day, remove the stamens and stuff with ricotta, then fry in a light tempura batter.

☞ Tofu

isn't to everyone's taste, but if you treat it as a blank canvas and are brave with your flavourings and textures, it can be transformed into something quite special. It's important to drain tofu well and pat it dry using kitchen paper, as you don't want any residual water to dilute your marinade or soften a golden crust. Use a feisty marinade, a thick sticky glaze, or coat in cornflour, batter or breadcrumbs to give a crisp crust. I like the way tofu readily takes on other flavours and can be adapted to suit different styles of cooking: it's perfect in Asian dishes, but also works in Western tomato-based dishes and hearty broths. Look out for smoked tofu (with sesame seeds is particularly good); silken tofu, which can be blended to make creamy sauces; and golden fried tofu that needs very little embellishment.

▶▶

Slices of rosemary- and garlic-marinated tofu are coated in breadcrumbs and fried until crisp and golden, then served with a punchy salsa. Any slightly stale bread (including crusts) can be turned into breadcrumbs, and I like to keep a ready supply in the freezer.

Tofu Escalopes with Salsa

Serves: 4   **Preparation time:** 20 minutes, plus 1 hour marinating
Cooking time: 12 minutes

450g/1lb firm tofu, drained, patted dry and
    sliced into 8 × 1cm/½in slices
2 eggs
75g/2½oz/1¼ cups day-old breadcrumbs or
    Japanese panko crumbs
finely grated zest of 1 large unwaxed lemon
5 tbsp sunflower oil
sea salt and freshly ground black pepper

MARINADE
2 tbsp extra virgin olive oil
2 large garlic cloves, crushed
1 heaped tbsp finely chopped rosemary leaves

TO SERVE
100g/3½oz/¾ cup drained tinned flageolet
    beans, or cooked dried flageolet beans
    (see pages 8–9)
1 recipe quantity Tomato and Chilli Salsa
    (see page 22)
juice of 1 large unwaxed lemon
rocket salad

1. Mix together the ingredients for the marinade and season well. Put the tofu in a large, shallow dish, spoon the marinade over and spread over both sides. Leave to marinate, covered, for 1 hour.

2. Meanwhile, mix the flageolet beans into the salsa, using the lemon juice instead of lime.

3. Beat the eggs in a shallow dish. Put the breadcrumbs and lemon zest in a separate shallow dish and season. Heat the sunflower oil in a large frying pan over a medium heat. Dip the tofu slices into the egg and then the crumbs until coated all over, then fry for 3 minutes on each side until golden (in two batches if necessary). Drain on kitchen paper and serve with the salsa and a rocket salad.

Pictured on page 41.

Smoked Tofu and Mango Salad

To make this zingy Asian-inspired salad, start with the dressing. Mix together **5 tbsp light olive oil**, **the juice of 1 lime** and **2 tsp peeled and finely chopped root ginger** and season with **salt and pepper**. Put **2 handfuls of rocket leaves** and **1 roughly chopped Little Gem lettuce** on a serving plate, then scatter over **½ diced red onion**, **6 thinly sliced radishes**, **1 deseeded and finely chopped medium red chilli** and **1 peeled mango, cubed**. Heat **1 tbsp light olive oil** in a large frying pan and fry **350g/12oz/3¼ cups cubed smoked tofu** for 3 minutes, turning once, until golden. Pour the dressing over the salad and toss until combined, then scatter over the smoked tofu and a **small handful of torn coriander leaves** and **chopped chives**.

Crispy Thai-Spiced Tofu

Mix together **3 tbsp cornflour**, **1 tbsp Thai 7-spice**, **1 tsp smoked mild paprika** and **salt and pepper** in a large, flat dish. Dunk **450g/1lb tofu** cut into 8 long 1cm/½in slices into the cornflour mixture until coated all over. Heat **150ml/5fl oz/⅔ cup sunflower oil** in a large, non-stick frying pan over a medium heat. Fry the tofu for 3–4 minutes each side until golden and crisp. Drain on kitchen paper. Serve sprinkled with **2 chopped spring onions**, **2 tbsp chopped coriander leaves** and **1 long red deseeded and chopped chilli**.

Tofu Bahn Mi

To make this Franco-Vietnamese baguette, mix together **3 tbsp rice vinegar** and **2 tsp clear honey** in a bowl and stir in **1 grated carrot** and a **5cm/2in piece of deseeded and shredded cucumber**. Mix together **2 tsp hot chilli sauce** and **2 tbsp soy sauce** in a dish. Add **300g/10½oz tofu**, cut into 4 × 1.5cm/⅝in slices. Season with **salt** and **pepper** and turn the tofu in the marinade. Leave the vegetables and tofu to marinate for at least 30 minutes. Fry the tofu in **4 tbsp sunflower oil** for 6 minutes, turning once, until crisp on both sides. Spread **4 small baguettes** with **mayonnaise** and top with **lettuce**, the drained carrot and cucumber mixture, the fried tofu, a **few coriander leaves** and an **extra splash of chilli sauce**, if you like.

Chapter 2
Pack of Pasta (and Noodles)

So simple, so versatile, so economical: a pack of pasta is the perfect foundation for many meat-free meals. In this chapter, it's at the heart of the Linguine Carbonara with Crispy Capers, Tagliatelle with Asparagus and Wild Garlic Pesto, and Creamy Porcini and Sea Beet Orzo. Let's not forget noodles, either, which are equally diverse. For starters, there's Wonton Ravioli with Rocket, Pho with Kale Chips, and Burmese Noodle, Tofu and Winter Greens Curry. All completely different dishes, yet with a common theme.

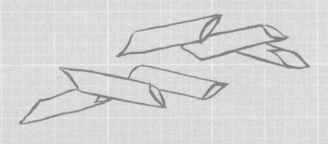

This Provençal soup, known as pistou, is great for using up bags of pasta lurking in the cupboard that don't quite hold enough for a whole meal but you don't want to go to waste, either. Feel free to swap the veg, depending on what you have to hand, and likewise the basil sauce can be made with a mixture of herbs, including oregano, thyme, marjoram and rocket.

Provençal Soup

Serves: 4   **Preparation time:** 15 minutes, plus making the stock
Cooking time: 20 minutes

1 heaped tbsp butter
2 leeks, sliced
2 carrots, diced
1 celery stick, sliced
1 fennel bulb, sliced
1 bouquet garni, made up of a large bay leaf
   and a few thyme and parsley sprigs
1l/35fl oz/4 cups Vegetable Stock
   (see page 14)
75g/2½oz spaghettini or dried pasta shape
   of choice
235g/8½oz/scant 2 cups drained tinned
   butter beans or cooked dried butter beans
   (see pages 8–9)

2 courgettes, quartered lengthways
   and sliced
55g/2oz/½ cup fresh shelled peas or
   frozen peas
4 thick slices of day-old country-style bread

BASIL SAUCE
4 large handfuls of basil leaves, plus extra
   to serve
2 garlic cloves
6 tbsp extra virgin olive oil
6 heaped tbsp finely grated vegetarian
   Parmesan cheese, plus extra to serve
sea salt and freshly ground black pepper

1. Melt the butter in a large, heavy-based saucepan over a medium heat. Add the leeks, carrots, celery, fennel and bouquet garni and cook for 10 minutes, stirring regularly, until softened.

2. Pour in the stock and bring to the boil. Add the pasta and gently boil for 5 minutes until almost tender, then add the butter beans, courgettes and peas and cook for another 5 minutes until tender.

3. Meanwhile, heat a ridged griddle pan over a high heat and griddle the bread until toasted on both sides and blackened in places.

4. To make the basil sauce, put the basil, garlic and oil in a blender and blend until smooth. Transfer to a bowl, stir in the Parmesan and season with salt and pepper. Taste, and add more Parmesan, if you like. Put a slice of toasted bread in each serving bowl – a wide, shallow one is best – and ladle the soup over, removing the bouquet garni first. Spoon the basil sauce on top and serve with extra Parmesan and basil leaves.

Don't throw away the rind from hard cheeses such as Parmesan, as they can be added to soups and stews to add an umami (savoury) richness to the broth.

If you are new to culinary gardening, try *growing your own herbs*. Seeds are more economical; young plants are quicker to establish. Start with oregano, thyme, basil, chives, rosemary, sage, coriander, mint, bay leaves and flat-leaf parsley. Mint is best grown in a container; coriander and basil need a sheltered sunny spot. Hardy bay, rosemary and sage provide fresh herbs throughout the year.

The taste of this pasta dish belies the fact that it's made from humble, simple ingredients. Even the aubergine skin does not go to waste, as it's cut into thin strips, fried until crisp and piled on top of the pasta just before serving.

Spaghetti with Aubergine, Cheese and Mint

Serves: 4   *Preparation time:* 15 minutes   *Cooking time:* 25 minutes

2 aubergines
4 tbsp extra virgin olive oil, plus extra
    for drizzling
400g/14oz dried spaghetti
1 onion, finely chopped
1 garlic clove, finely chopped
4 tomatoes, deseeded and chopped

1 tbsp tomato purée
125g/4½oz/1 cup drained tinned chickpeas or
    cooked dried chickpeas (see pages 8–9)
1 handful of mint leaves
sea salt and freshly ground black pepper
40g/1½oz mature vegetarian sheep's cheese,
    grated, to serve

1. Using a vegetable peeler, remove the skin from the aubergines in strips. Cut the skin into thin strips and dice the flesh. Heat the oil in a large, deep frying pan over a medium heat and fry the aubergine skin for 2–3 minutes until crisp, then remove using a slotted spoon and drain on kitchen paper. Add the diced aubergine to the pan and fry for 8 minutes, or until light golden all over.

2. Meanwhile, bring a large pan of salted water to the boil and cook the spaghetti following the pack instructions. Drain, reserving 6 tablespoons of the cooking water.

3. Add the onion to the aubergine and cook for another 8 minutes until softened, then add the garlic, tomatoes, tomato purée and chickpeas. Cook over a medium-low heat for 5 minutes, stirring often and adding enough of the reserved pasta cooking water to loosen the mixture and make a sauce.

4. Just before serving, stir in the mint and season with salt and pepper. Spoon the sauce on top of the pasta, drizzle with a little extra oil and serve with the fried aubergine skin and cheese piled on top.

Freeze tomato purée in teaspoon-sized piles on a baking sheet until solid. Transfer to a zip-lock bag when frozen and return to the freezer to use as needed.

This is one of my favourite summer pasta dishes. It's light, quick, full of flavour and became a mainstay meal at home one summer as it admirably used up a glut of courgettes (see page 39). Walnut pieces are cheaper than halved or whole nuts, and are perfect for the dish, saving you preparation time.

Courgette, Feta and Walnut Cavatappi

Serves: 4   **Preparation time:** 15 minutes   **Cooking time:** 15 minutes

400g/14oz dried cavatappi or pasta shape
   of choice
4 tbsp extra virgin olive oil
4 spring onions, chopped, green and white
   parts kept separate
2 large garlic cloves, finely chopped
1 red chilli, deseeded and chopped
3 courgettes, coarsely grated

juice and finely grated zest of
   2 unwaxed lemons
125g/4½oz feta cheese, cut into pieces
75g/2½oz/scant ½ cup walnut pieces,
   toasted (see page 18)
1 handful of basil or oregano leaves, torn
sea salt and freshly ground black pepper

1. Bring a large pan of salted water to the boil and cook the pasta following the pack instructions. Drain, reserving 4 tablespoons of the cooking water, and return the pasta to the pan.

2. Meanwhile, heat the oil in a large frying pan over a medium-low heat. Add the white part of the spring onions, the garlic and the chilli and fry for 2 minutes until softened but not browned. Add the courgettes and lemon zest and cook for another minute, then pour in the reserved pasta cooking water and lemon juice and heat through briefly.

3. Add the courgette mixture to the cooked pasta. Season with salt and pepper and toss until combined. Serve with the green part of the spring onions, the feta, the toasted walnuts and the herbs scattered over the top.

A handful of ingredients are transformed into a satisfying dish. Keep any spare chilli oil for frying eggs, salad dressings or stirring into noodles. Store in a sterilized jar (see page 11) in a cool, dark place.

Rigatoni with Golden Lemon Crumbs

Serves: 4   **Preparation time:** 10 minutes, plus at least 30 minutes infusing
Cooking time: 15 minutes

400g/14oz dried rigatoni
50g/1¾oz/¾ cup day-old breadcrumbs
finely grated zest of 1 large unwaxed lemon
5 large handfuls of curly kale, tough stalks
    removed, leaves shredded
3 large garlic cloves, finely chopped
sea salt and freshly ground black pepper

2 tbsp sunflower seeds, toasted (see page 18),
    to serve (optional)

CHILLI OIL
125ml/4fl oz/½ cup extra virgin olive oil
8–10 small dried chillies (quantity will
    depend on their heat)

1. To make the chilli oil, pour the oil into a small pan, add the chillies and heat gently for 5 minutes. Remove from the heat and leave to infuse for at least 30 minutes.

2. Bring a large pan of salted water to the boil and cook the pasta. Drain, reserving 100ml/3½fl oz/scant ½ cup of the cooking water. Return the pasta and reserved cooking water to the pan.

3. Meanwhile, heat 1 tablespoon of the chilli oil in a large, deep frying pan over a medium heat. Add the breadcrumbs and fry for 4 minutes, turning them regularly, until light golden and crisp. Stir in the lemon zest and briefly heat through, then tip into a bowl.

4. Add 3 more tablespoons of chilli oil to the frying pan and heat over a medium heat. Add the kale and stir-fry for 3–4 minutes until tender. Add the garlic and cook for 1 minute. Transfer the kale to the pasta pan and toss. Season and sprinkle with the lemon breadcrumbs and sunflower seeds, if using.

Instead of throwing away stale bread, blitz it – crusts and all – in a grinder or small food processor until you have coarse and/or fine crumbs. Store the breadcrumbs in an airtight container in the freezer for up to 3 months, and use straight from frozen.

Capers aren't to everyone's taste – in fact I'm not a huge fan of them myself – but when fried until crisp they add a delicious piquant salty bite, in perfect contrast to the creaminess of the carbonara sauce. Do try this, as they really are something else when cooked in this way.

Linguine Carbonara with Crispy Capers

Serves: 4   *Preparation time:* 5 minutes   *Cooking time:* 15 minutes

400g/14oz dried linguine
1 tbsp olive oil
5 tbsp bottled capers, drained, rinsed and patted dry
40g/1½oz butter
3 vine-ripened tomatoes, deseeded and diced
2 large garlic cloves, finely chopped

100g/3½oz vegetarian Parmesan cheese, grated
3 large eggs, lightly beaten
1 tbsp chopped oregano leaves or 2 tsp dried oregano
sea salt and freshly ground black pepper

1. Bring a large pan of salted water to the boil and cook the pasta following the pack instructions.

2. Meanwhile, heat the oil in a large, deep frying pan over a medium heat. Add the capers, turn the heat down slightly and fry for 3–4 minutes, turning occasionally, until golden and crisp, then drain on kitchen paper. Add the butter to the pan and when melted, stir in the tomatoes and garlic and cook for 3 minutes until softened, taking care that the garlic doesn't burn.

3. Mix three-quarters of the Parmesan into the beaten eggs. When the pasta is cooked, use tongs to transfer it to the frying pan and reserve the pasta cooking water. Take the frying pan off the heat and quickly pour in the egg mixture. Using tongs, turn the linguine so it becomes evenly coated in the egg mixture, which should thicken without scrambling. Add 2–4 tablespoons of the pasta cooking water, if needed, to keep the pasta moist and to give a glossy sauce. Serve seasoned with pepper and sprinkled with the remaining Parmesan and oregano.

Give tomatoes a good sniff before buying, and if they don't smell of tomatoes, give them a miss as they won't taste of anything either. Store tomatoes at room temperature – the cold of the fridge will affect their taste and texture, turning the flesh mealy and suppressing the flavour.

Homemade pesto takes a matter of minutes and is fresher and cheaper than shop-bought, especially with foraged ingredients. Pesto can be so much more than the classic Ligurian basil version, and adapted to suit seasonal ingredients. Wild garlic leaves have just enough garlicky flavour without being too overpowering, and if you do manage to discover a sizeable patch, make a double batch of pesto and freeze it. Pine nuts can vary in quality, so try almonds, cashews, walnuts or Brazils, for a sweet, nutty creaminess.

Tagliatelle with Asparagus and Wild Garlic Pesto

Serves: 4   *Preparation time:* 10 minutes   *Cooking time:* 15 minutes

400g/14oz dried tagliatelle
150g/5½oz asparagus tips, trimmed

WILD GARLIC PESTO
2 large handfuls of wild garlic leaves, flowers
   (if any) reserved (or use chive flowers)

1 handful of blanched almonds
100ml/3½fl oz/scant ½ cup mild-flavoured
   extra virgin olive oil, plus extra for topping
1 handful of finely grated vegetarian
   Parmesan cheese, plus extra to serve
sea salt and freshly ground black pepper

1. Bring a large pan of salted water to the boil and cook the pasta following the pack instructions. Add the asparagus about 3 minutes before the pasta is ready. Drain, reserving 4 tablespoons of the pasta cooking water, and return the cooked pasta and asparagus to the pan.

2. Meanwhile, make the pesto. Put the wild garlic leaves and almonds in a mini food processor (or use a stick blender and a beaker) and process until finely chopped. Continue to blend, adding the oil in two batches, and the Parmesan, then season with salt and pepper. Spoon the pesto into a bowl or jar and drizzle some extra olive oil over the top. (It will keep for up to 3 days in the fridge.)

3. Add as much pesto and reserved cooking water as needed to coat the pasta and asparagus, then turn the pasta until it is evenly coated. Taste and add extra salt and pepper, if needed. Serve sprinkled with more Parmesan and wild garlic flowers, if you have them.

Use leftover cooked long pasta to make a frittata. Just stir the pasta into the egg mixture with a handful of grated Pecorino, and cook following the instructions on page 119.

Wild garlic

makes an excellent alternative to garlic or chives in dishes, and is best left raw or lightly cooked. You can find wild garlic (you'll probably be able to smell it before you see it) with its broad, spear-like leaves in woody areas, hedge banks or waysides. The plant also has delicate white flowers on top of a thin stem — both leaves and flowers are edible.

I'd walked past small clumps of **sea beet leaves** on a local beach for years and never really considered that they could be edible. However, when I tried them I found that they had a *taste reminiscent of spinach* — but with none of that tartness you might expect. Make sure that you pick the young leaves, keep away from where dogs may have been and wash well before use.

O.K, dried porcini may be pricey on the face of it, but a little goes a long way and the soaking water also turns into a wonderful, rich stock. Orzo is a small, rice-shaped pasta and makes a good alternative to grains. There's something very comforting and humble about orzo, which is also featured in the Scamorza, Orzo and Basil Oil Salad (see page 151) – it might be worth cooking up double the quantity. If you can't find sea beet (see opposite), you could use spinach, kale, cavolo nero or chard instead.

Creamy Porcini and Sea Beet Orzo

Serves: 4   *Preparation time:* 10 minutes, plus making the stock and 20 minutes soaking   *Cooking time:* 25 minutes

25g/1oz/¼ cup dried porcini
3 tbsp olive oil
280g/10oz chestnut mushrooms, sliced
150g/5½oz sea beet, spinach or chard, stalks
  thinly sliced and leaves shredded
2 tsp thyme leaves or 1 tsp dried thyme

350ml/12fl oz/scant 1½ cups Vegetable Stock
  (see page 14)
125ml/4fl oz/½ cup crème fraîche
400g/14oz/3 cups orzo pasta
sea salt and freshly ground black pepper
grated vegetarian Parmesan cheese, to serve

1. Put the porcini in a bowl and cover with 200ml/7fl oz/scant 1 cup just-boiled water. Leave to soak for 20 minutes until softened. Strain the mushrooms, reserving the soaking liquid.

2. Heat the olive oil in a large, deep frying pan over a medium heat. Add the soaked porcini and fry for 5 minutes until slightly crisp. Add the fresh mushrooms and continue to cook for another 5 minutes, stirring regularly, until starting to colour and turn crisp. The fresh mushrooms will appear dry at first and will then release liquid, which you want to cook out otherwise they will be soggy. Stir in the sea beet stalks and thyme and cook for another 2 minutes.

3. Pour in the stock and soaking liquid (leaving any gritty bits in the bottom of the bowl) and bring to the boil, then turn the heat down to low. Add the sea beet leaves and simmer for 5–7 minutes until reduced by a third. Stir in the crème fraîche and simmer for another 2 minutes until slightly reduced.

4. Meanwhile, cook the orzo in a large saucepan of boiling salted water following the pack instructions. Drain, reserving 6 tablespoons of the cooking water. Add the cooked orzo to the mushroom sauce with enough of the reserved pasta cooking water to make a fairly loose sauce, then turn until everything is mixed together. Season with salt and pepper and serve sprinkled with Parmesan.

Another recipe using porcini is Rainbow Chard and Parmesan Tortino (see page 128).

Tahini, a thick paste made from ground sesame seeds, is traditionally used in hummus, but I like the nutty creaminess it gives the stock for this Japanese-inspired noodle dish. As a bonus, tahini is a valuable source of protein. Sprinkle the wild garlic flowers over the broth just before serving.

Udon Noodle Pot with Tahini and Wild Garlic

Serves: 4   **Preparation time:** *20 minutes, plus making the stock*
Cooking time: *10 minutes*

4 tbsp light soy sauce
2 tsp caster sugar
½ tsp dried chilli flakes
1 tbsp grated root ginger, peeled
2 heaped tbsp light tahini
600ml/21fl oz/scant 2½ cups Vegetable Stock (see page 14)
1 handful of wild garlic, leaves cut crossways into strips, flowers reserved (if any)
2 tbsp sunflower oil

1 large onion, sliced
300g/10½oz mixed mushrooms, such as shiitake, chestnut or oyster, sliced
2 pak choi, white parts thinly sliced and leaves thickly sliced
800g/1¾lb soft udon noodles
sea salt and freshly ground black pepper
Crispy Onions and Ginger (see page 23), to serve (optional)

For foraging wild garlic, see page 55.

1. Mix together the soy sauce, sugar, chilli flakes, ginger and tahini in a saucepan until combined. Pour in the stock and reserved noodle cooking water and heat slowly until hot, stirring occasionally. (Do not overheat the tahini stock or it may curdle.) Stir in the wild garlic leaves and leave to one side.

2. Heat the oil in a large wok and stir-fry the onion for 3 minutes until softened slightly. Add the mushrooms and the white part of the pak choi and stir-fry for another 5 minutes, then add the green part of the pak choi and stir-fry for a final 2 minutes until the mushrooms are starting to crisp up and the leaves are tender but still crisp.

3. Meanwhile, bring a large pan of water to the boil and cook the noodles following the pack instructions. Drain the noodles and divide into four large, shallow bowls. Ladle the stock over the noodles and top with the mushroom mixture. Sprinkle with the wild garlic flowers, if using, and Crispy Onions and Ginger, if you like.

Wonton wrappers are used as an alternative to pasta to make ravioli. And, continuing the fusion theme, the wonton parcels are filled with Edamame and Wasabi Hummus (see page 32). Serve with a buttery ginger sauce.

Wonton Ravioli with Rocket

Serves: 4   *Preparation time:* 20 minutes, plus making the hummus
Cooking time: 20 minutes

40 square wonton wrappers for steaming
  (rather than frying), about 1½ packs
¾ recipe quantity Edamame and Wasabi
  Hummus (see page 32)
1–2 tsp sea salt, to taste
100g/3½oz butter
4cm/1½in piece of root ginger, peeled,
  finely grated and juice squeezed out

juice of ½ lime
1 handful of roughly chopped toasted walnuts
  (see page 18)
1 heaped tbsp snipped chives
1 handful of rocket leaves
freshly ground black pepper

1. To make the ravioli, lay half of the wonton wrappers on a large sheet of baking parchment. Spoon a tablespoon of the hummus into the middle of each one and brush the edges of the wrappers with water. Top each one with a second wonton wrapper and press the edges together to seal. Turn the ravioli over so they are resting on their tops to prevent them sticking to the paper.

2. Fill a large, deep frying pan with water, add the salt and bring to the boil. Cook the ravioli in four batches for 3–5 minutes until the wontons are tender, keeping each batch warm on a large covered warm plate.

3. Meanwhile, to make the sauce, melt the butter in a pan. Add the ginger juice and cook over a low heat for 2 minutes to infuse, then season with salt and pepper. Spoon the ginger butter over the ravioli and serve with a squeeze of lime juice and scattered with the walnuts, chives and rocket.

Wonton wrappers can be found frozen or chilled in Asian stores and some supermarkets; there are those suited to steaming, while others need to be fried. I like to keep a pack in the freezer as they take little time to defrost and are great for making dumplings, crisps or, as here, as a wrap.

For a bit of crunch, I've topped this Vietnamese noodle soup with kale chips, reminiscent of the crispy seaweed you find in Chinese restaurants and delicious sprinkled over rice or noodles, or enjoyed as a nutritious snack.

Pho with Kale Chips

Serves: 4   **Preparation time:** *15 minutes, plus making the stock*
Cooking time: *20 minutes*

1 recipe quantity Asian Stock (see page 15)
175g/6oz baby spinach leaves
1 long red chilli, deseeded and thinly
    sliced diagonally
3 spring onions, thinly sliced diagonally,
    green and white parts kept separate
1 tsp sesame oil
2 tbsp light soy sauce
250g/9oz thick dried rice noodles
2 carrots, cut into thin julienne strips
1 small red pepper, cut into julienne strips

2 tbsp roughly chopped coriander leaves
2 tbsp roughly chopped mint leaves
sea salt and freshly ground black pepper
2 tsp sesame seeds, toasted, to serve

KALE CHIPS
1 tbsp sesame oil
1 tsp light soy sauce
3 large handfuls of curly kale, larger stalks
    removed, leaves torn into large pieces
    if necessary

1. To make the kale chips, preheat the oven to 160°C/315°F/Gas 3. Mix together the sesame oil and soy sauce in a large bowl. Add the kale, and toss with your hands until coated. Scatter the kale over a large baking sheet in an even layer. Bake for 15–20 minutes, turning once or twice, until crisp but still green. Transfer the kale to a bowl and leave to one side.

2. Meanwhile, pour the Asian stock into a large saucepan and bring to the boil over a medium heat, then leave to bubble away for 3 minutes. Strain and discard the flavourings, then return the stock to the pan and add the spinach, half the chilli and the white part of the spring onions. Turn the heat down slightly and simmer for 3 minutes until the spinach has wilted.

3. Stir in the sesame oil and soy sauce and season with pepper (the stock should be salty enough, but you can add salt if you like) and heat through briefly.

4. Cook the rice noodles until tender, then drain and refresh under cold running water. Divide the noodles, carrots, red pepper, green part of the spring onions, coriander and mint into four large, shallow bowls. Ladle the stock over, sprinkle with the sesame seeds and put a pile of the kale chips in the middle of each bowl.

Store fresh chillies, lemongrass, kaffir lime leaves and curry leaves in an airtight container or small zip-lock bag in the freezer. There's no need to defrost before use.

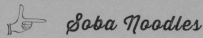 ## Soba Noodles

These thin, grey-brown, dried Japanese noodles come in two types: those made with buckwheat flour, which are gluten-free; and those made with a combination of wheat and buckwheat, which are slightly more robust. I've also spotted a version made with green tea powder, though the tea adds colour rather than much flavour. When cooking soba, follow the instructions on the pack to avoid the noodles overcooking and becoming sticky or even falling apart. When draining, follow the Japanese practice of reserving some of the cooking water. This is called sobayu and is sometimes added to the broth or dipping sauce or drunk as a soup. Refresh cooked noodles under cold running water to cool them quickly and get rid of excess starch, which can make them sticky and slimy. Soba can be served warm or cold in noodle salads or broths, or with a soy-based dipping sauce. They can be briefly stir-fried, but it's not ideal as they have a tendency to fall apart. If you want to reheat them, put them in a colander and pour over a just-boiled kettleful of water — that should just be enough to warm them up.

Burma (Myanmar) is bordered by China, Thailand and India, so it's not unusual to find a mix of influences in a dish. Don't be put off by the list of ingredients; this fragrant curry is easy to make.

Burmese Noodle, Tofu and Winter Greens Curry

Serves: 4   **Preparation time:** *20 minutes, plus making the stock*
Cooking time: *25 minutes*

4 tbsp mild curry powder
400g/14oz firm tofu, drained, patted dry and
   cut into large bite-sized cubes
1 onion, cut into wedges
3 large garlic cloves, peeled
2.5cm/1in piece of root ginger, peeled
   and quartered
4 tbsp sunflower oil
400g/14fl oz/scant 1⅔ cups coconut milk
300ml/10½fl oz/scant 1¼ cups Vegetable Stock
   (see page 14)
2 tbsp light soy sauce

½ tsp dried chilli flakes or 1 medium red
   chilli, sliced
2 lemongrass sticks, bruised
1 tbsp soft brown sugar
1 red pepper, deseeded and chopped
4 large handfuls of winter greens or curly
   kale, stalks removed, leaves shredded
200g/7oz dried soba noodles
1 handful of coriander leaves, chopped
sea salt and freshly ground black pepper
lime wedges, to serve

1. Sprinkle half the curry powder over a plate and season with salt and pepper. Lightly dust the tofu in the curry powder and leave to one side.

2. Put the onion, garlic, ginger and half the oil in a mini food processor and process to a paste. Scrape the paste into a large, heavy-based saucepan and cook over a medium heat for 2 minutes, stirring continuously. Add the coconut milk, stock, soy sauce, chilli and lemongrass and bring up to boiling point, then stir in the sugar. Turn the heat down slightly and simmer, part-covered, for 15 minutes until reduced and thickened. Add the remaining curry powder, the red pepper and the winter greens. Season with pepper, then cook, stirring occasionally, for 5 minutes until tender.

3. Meanwhile, heat the remaining oil in a large, non-stick frying pan and fry the tofu in two batches over a medium heat for 6 minutes, turning occasionally, until golden. Drain on kitchen paper. Cook the noodles following the pack instructions, drain and divide into four large, shallow bowls. Spoon the curry over the top, followed by the tofu, and scatter with the coriander before serving with wedges of lime.

Freeze any leftover coconut milk in ice cube trays or a plastic container with a lid. Tip out into a small plastic bag, secure the top and freeze for up to 3 months.

Pictured on page 63.

Soba, Sea Vegetable and Radish Salad

Cook **165g/5¾oz dried soba noodles** following the pack instructions, then drain and refresh under cold running water. Put them in a large serving bowl and add **100g/3½oz cooked and cooled edamame beans**, **10 thinly sliced radishes** and a **6cm/2½in piece deseeded and diced cucumber**. Lightly toast **1 tbsp sesame seeds** and **3 tbsp mixed sea vegetable salad** in a dry frying pan for 2 minutes, shaking the pan regularly, until the seaweed is crisp. To make the dressing, mix **4 tbsp rice vinegar, 2 tsp soy sauce, 2 tsp sesame oil, 5 tbsp sunflower oil, 1 tsp peeled and finely chopped root ginger** and **1 small finely chopped garlic clove**. Season with **salt** and **pepper** and spoon the dressing over the noodle salad. Sprinkle with the vegetable mix, and serve.

Soba with Miso Sauce

It's worth making double the quantity of this sauce, as it will keep for up to 1 week in an airtight container in the fridge. Serve it warm or cold as a dressing for salads, a stir-fry sauce or spooned over cooked rice or pasta. Cook **225g/8oz dried soba noodles** following the pack instructions, then drain and refresh under cold running water. To make the sauce, combine **5 tbsp mirin** and **1 heaped tbsp caster sugar** in a small pan and bring to the boil, then turn the heat down and simmer for 2 minutes, stirring until the sugar dissolves. Mix together **6 tbsp water, 4 tbsp brown rice miso** and **1 tbsp English mustard**, then stir into the pan. Pour boiling water over the noodles and divide into four large, shallow bowls, then pour the sauce over and turn until coated. Sprinkle with **chopped coriander** and **toasted sesame seeds**, or serve with stir-fried vegetables or fried tofu.

Soba with Coriander Dressing

Cook **250g/9oz dried soba noodles** following the pack instructions, then drain and refresh under cold running water. Combine **2 handfuls of fresh coriander leaves, 2 large garlic cloves, 1 long red chilli, 5cm/2in piece of peeled and chopped root ginger**, finely grated zest and juice of **2 limes, 5 tbsp sunflower oil, 2 tbsp light soy sauce, 1 tsp caster sugar** and **1 tbsp toasted sesame oil** in a mini food processor or blender and process to a thick paste. Spoon the dressing over warm or cold noodles.

Chapter 3
Sack of Rice
(and Other Grains)

Reputedly the most widely eaten food on the planet, rice is so much more than just an accompaniment. There are numerous varieties to choose from, such as the creamy risotto rice used here in the Arancini Eggs, or jasmine rice, which goes to make the Thai Rice with Spiced Cashews. And let's not forget the numerous other grains, which are equally versatile and economical. Try them in the Barley, Squash and Wild Oregano Risotto or the Quinoa and Roasted Peanut Salad.

This is a cross between the Italian arancini (fried rice ball) and a meat-free version of the British Scotch egg. It came about when a friend gave me some eggs from her prolific hens and I had some leftover risotto in the fridge that needed eating. This marriage of dishes was pure guesswork, but I'm pleased to say that it's a happy union!

Arancini Eggs

Serves: 4   *Preparation time:* 10 minutes   *Cooking time:* 15 minutes

5 eggs (1 lightly beaten)
3 tbsp finely grated vegetarian Parmesan cheese
375g/13oz leftover risotto (or ⅓ recipe quantity
   Last-of-the-Beans Risotto, see page 81,
   leaving out the broad beans and Dolcelatte)

75g/2½oz/1¼ cups day-old breadcrumbs
4 tbsp plain flour
sunflower oil, for deep-frying
sea salt and freshly ground black pepper

1. Put 4 of the eggs in a pan of cold water and bring to the boil, then turn the heat down slightly and gently boil the eggs for 5 minutes. Drain the eggs, cool under cold running water, then peel.

2. Meanwhile, stir the Parmesan into the risotto rice and season with salt and pepper. Beat the remaining egg in a shallow bowl. Tip the breadcrumbs and flour into two separate shallow bowls.

3. Take a quarter of the risotto mixture and press it out in an even layer in the palm of your hand. Lightly dust one of the eggs in the flour, then put it in the centre of the risotto. Wrap the risotto around the egg in an even layer and press the edges together to make a ball. Dust the wrapped egg in the flour and pat away any excess, then dip into the beaten egg and roll in the breadcrumbs. Repeat to make 4 balls in total.

4. Heat enough oil in a deep pan to deep-fry the Arancini eggs. (It is hot enough when a small piece of bread turns golden and crisp in 30 seconds.) Deep-fry 2 eggs at a time for 4–5 minutes, turning them occasionally until golden and crisp all over. Drain on kitchen paper, and repeat to cook the remaining eggs. Serve warm.

Don't throw away leftover oil from deep-frying – instead, leave it to cool, then strain into an airtight jar and store in a dark, cool place. It can be used for up to 2 weeks. Alternatively, the oil can be poured into a freezer-proof container and frozen for up to 3 months.

Radishes

are great for newcomers to vegetable growing, as they're easy to grow, tolerant of most soil types and take a mere 4 weeks to crop. They come in all shapes and sizes – from spherical to long and thin – and in colours ranging from red and cream to pink and white. Sow the seeds at weekly intervals for a ready supply of this crisp, slightly fiery vegetable throughout the summer.

With its nutty flavour and texture, buckwheat makes a more substantial addition to grain-based salads than couscous or quinoa. It's a bit of an intruder in the grain family, though, as it's actually a seed – however, it's often used in the same way as wheat so it deserves its place here.

Buckwheat and Sour Cherry Salad

Serves: 4　*Preparation time:* 15 minutes　*Cooking time:* 25 minutes

140g/5oz/²⁄₃ cup buckwheat groats
　　or bulgur wheat
juice of ½ small orange
1 tsp heaped clear honey
3 tbsp rice vinegar
1 handful of dried sour cherries,
　　halved if large
6 radishes, sliced into rounds

1 small red or pink onion, diced
2 handfuls of mint leaves, chopped
2 handfuls of parsley leaves, chopped
2 tbsp extra virgin olive oil
1 large handful of unsalted, shelled pistachio
　　nuts, toasted (see page 18)
100g/3½oz feta cheese, crumbled
sea salt and freshly ground black pepper

1. Toast the buckwheat in a frying pan over a medium heat for 3 minutes, turning the grains occasionally, until they smell toasted. Transfer to a saucepan and cover with water. Bring to the boil over a medium heat, then turn the heat down to low and part-cover the pan. Cook for 18–20 minutes, or until the buckwheat is soft, yet remains chewy.

2. Meanwhile, whisk the orange juice, honey and rice vinegar together in a small pan. Bring to the boil and add the sour cherries, then turn the heat off and leave the cherries to steep for 15 minutes.

3. Drain the buckwheat well and tip into a serving bowl with the radishes, onion, mint and parsley. Strain the sour cherries, reserving the juice mixture, and add them to the bowl. Whisk the olive oil into the juice mixture and pour into the bowl, then season with salt and pepper. Toss the salad until combined, then scatter the pistachios and feta over the top just before serving at room temperature.

If you use nuts, seeds, grains and pulses regularly it's best to buy them in bulk – in large packs – to keep costs down. Do check the use-by date on a regular basis, though, as they will deteriorate over time.

This is almost an Asian version of tabbouleh. As with the classic tabbouleh, its success lies in getting the balance right between the grain and the flavourings. The herbs should be dominant, as the coriander is here; a very high proportion of grains makes for a dull salad. I love the combination of crisp onions and ginger, roasted peanuts and soft herbs with the slightly salty soy dressing. I've used red quinoa for its colour more than anything else; go for whichever type you can buy easily.

Quinoa and Roasted Peanut Salad

Serves: 4　**Preparation time:** 10 minutes　**Cooking time:** 10 minutes

55g/2oz/scant ⅓ cup red quinoa
1 tbsp rapeseed oil
60g/2¼oz/heaped ⅓ cup whole
　unsalted peanuts
1 large handful of coriander, leaves and
　stalks finely chopped
1 tbsp sesame seeds, toasted (see page 18)
3 tbsp Crispy Onions and Ginger (see page 23)

DRESSING
1 tsp tamari or light soy sauce
2 tbsp rapeseed oil
½ tsp sugar
sea salt and freshly ground black pepper

1. Put the quinoa in a pan, cover with water and bring to the boil. Turn the heat down and simmer, part-covered, for 10 minutes until tender. Drain and leave to one side.

2. Meanwhile, heat the oil in a large frying pan over a medium heat. Turn the heat to medium-low, add the peanuts and fry for 2–3 minutes, turning once, until toasted. Remove with a slotted spoon, drain on kitchen paper and leave to cool.

3. Mix together the ingredients for the dressing and season with salt and pepper. Put the coriander leaves and stalks in a bowl with the quinoa, peanuts and sesame seeds. Pour the dressing over and toss until combined. Serve with the Crispy Onions and Ginger sprinkled over the top.

Serve with the Pea and Tofu Fritters (see page 162).

Don't discard the stalks from coriander or parsley, as they contain plenty of flavour and can be added to dishes where a slight crunch is not an issue, such as in this salad.

This is so adaptable. Go easy on the additions and serve it as a side dish to the Moroccan Slow-Cooked Vegetables (see page 159) or with the Pomegranate Salsa (see page 21), or pimp it up with extra cheese or a fried egg to make a main meal.

Feta and Pumpkin Seed Pilaff

Serves: 4   **Preparation time:** *15 minutes, plus making the stock and 10 minutes standing*   **Cooking time:** *25 minutes*

2 tbsp sunflower oil
1 onion, finely chopped
3 garlic cloves, finely chopped
8 cloves
6 cardamom pods, split
1 tbsp cumin seeds
½ tsp dried chilli flakes
300g/10½oz/1½ cups basmati rice
1 heaped tsp turmeric

750–800ml/26–28fl oz/3–scant 3½ cups
    Vegetable Stock (see page 14)
3 handfuls of spinach, tough stalks
    removed, leaves shredded
120g/4¼oz/1 cup drained tinned butter
    beans or cooked dried butter beans
    (see pages 8–9)
3 tbsp pumpkin seeds, toasted (see page 18)
100g/3½oz feta cheese, crumbled
sea salt and freshly ground black pepper

1. Heat the oil in a medium, deep frying pan over a medium heat. Add the onion and fry for 6 minutes until softened, then add the garlic, cloves, cardamom, cumin and chilli flakes and cook for 2 minutes.

2. Stir in the rice and turmeric, then pour in the stock; it should cover the rice by about 1cm/½in. Bring to the boil, then turn the heat down to its lowest setting, cover with a lid and and cook for 5 minutes.

3. Briefly remove the lid and stir in the spinach and butter beans, then return the lid and cook for another 10 minutes, or until the rice is tender and the stock has been absorbed. (Add more stock if the rice is not cooked, cover with the lid again and cook for a few more minutes until tender.) Season to taste with salt and pepper and leave to stand for 10 minutes. Serve the rice in bowls, sprinkled with the pumpkin seeds and feta cheese.

Leftover cooked rice can be kept in the fridge for up to 2 days or frozen; either way make sure you reheat it really well.

This is my take on the signature Korean rice dish, traditionally topped with seven different vegetables and a raw egg, which cooks in the heat of the rice. I like to vary the vegetables and prefer a soft-boiled egg or thin strips of omelette. A spoonful of Kimchi (see page 20) is not to be forgotten!

Bibimbap

Serves: 4 **Preparation time:** *20 minutes, plus making the stock*
Cooking time: *20 minutes*

400g/14oz/scant 2 cups short-grain brown
 rice, rinsed
4 large eggs
2 tbsp vegetable oil
250g/9oz chestnut mushrooms, sliced
2 carrots, cut into thin strips
2 courgettes, cut into thin strips
200g/7oz young spinach leaves, tough stalks
 removed (or use 8 portions of frozen
 whole-leaf spinach)

5 spring onions, finely chopped
3 garlic cloves, finely chopped
1 tbsp sesame seeds, toasted (see page 18)
3 tbsp light soy sauce
1 tsp sesame oil
200ml/7fl oz/scant 1 cup Vegetable Stock
 (see page 14)
sea salt and freshly ground black pepper
Kimchi (see page 20), to serve

1. Put the rice in a saucepan, pour in enough cold water to cover by 1cm/½in and season with salt. Bring to the boil, then turn the heat down to its lowest setting and cover. Simmer for 20 minutes, or until the rice is tender and the water has been absorbed. Leave the rice to stand on the warm hob until ready to serve.

2. Meanwhile, soft-boil the eggs for 4 minutes, cool briefly under cold running water, then peel and leave to one side. While the eggs are cooking, heat the vegetable oil in a large wok over a high heat and stir-fry the mushrooms for 4 minutes until starting to turn golden. Leave to one side.

3. Steam the carrots and courgettes for 2–3 minutes, keeping them separate, until just tender. Cook the spinach with a splash of water for 2–3 minutes until tender. Transfer all the vegetables to a large, warm plate and cover to keep them warm.

4. Put the spring onions, garlic, sesame seeds, soy sauce, sesame oil and vegetable stock in a small pan and simmer over a medium-low heat for 2 minutes, then season with pepper.

5. Divide the rice into four warm bowls and spoon over two-thirds of the hot stock mixture. Top with the vegetables, keeping each one in a separate pile. Spoon the remaining stock mixture over the top. Cut each egg in half and put in the centre. Serve immediately with the Kimchi.

I always keep a bag of frozen spinach in the freezer. Look for whole-leaf spinach rather than chopped, which has a tendency to turn to mush when cooked.

Calendula (pot marigold) was once known as 'poor man's saffron', as its dried petals look remarkably similar to strands of saffron but at a fraction of the price. Soak the dried petals briefly to release their golden colour.

Paella with Poor Man's Saffron

Serves: *4*   **Preparation time:** *15 minutes, plus making the stock, 30 minutes soaking and 10 minutes standing*   **Cooking time:** *35 minutes*

2 heaped tsp dried pot marigold petals
   (see opposite)
165g/5¾oz/1½ cups frozen petits pois
3 tbsp rapeseed or olive oil
1 large onion, chopped
2 large peppers, 1 red and 1 yellow,
   deseeded and chopped
3 garlic cloves, chopped
280g/10oz/1½ cups paella rice
2 tsp smoked mild paprika
1 tsp turmeric

4 tbsp sherry, or extra vegetable stock
1.2l/40fl oz/4¾ cups Vegetable Stock
   (see page 14)
2 tomatoes, deseeded and diced
2 handfuls of small black pitted olives
sea salt and freshly ground black pepper

SMOKED PAPRIKA ALMONDS
1 tbsp rapeseed or olive oil
75g/2½oz/½ cup blanched whole almonds
1 heaped tsp smoked mild paprika

1. Soak the marigold petals in 4 tablespoons warm water for 30 minutes. Meanwhile, let the petits pois defrost in a bowl. Heat the oil in a paella pan or large, non-stick, deep frying pan with a lid over a medium heat. Add the onion and fry for 5 minutes until softened but not coloured. Add the peppers and cook for another 3 minutes, then add the garlic and cook until the peppers have softened.

2. Add the rice, smoked paprika and turmeric and turn to coat them in the onions. Pour in the sherry, if using, and let it bubble away until the alcohol evaporates, then pour in the stock and marigold petals and soaking liquid, season, stir and bring to the boil. Turn the heat down to low and leave the rice to cook without stirring for 15 minutes.

3. Scatter over the peas, tomatoes and olives and press into the rice with the back of a spoon. Do not stir the rice; you want the bottom to form a crust. Cook for another 5 minutes until the rice is tender and the stock mostly absorbed. Remove from the heat, cover and leave to stand for 10 minutes.

4. Meanwhile, heat the oil in a frying pan over a medium heat and fry the almonds for 3 minutes, shaking occasionally, until they start to colour. Add the paprika and season with salt, turn the nuts to coat and cook for another 2 minutes. Tip out onto a plate. Serve the paella scattered with the paprika almonds.

Poor man's saffron is also used in Moroccan Slow-Cooked Vegetables (see page 159).

Pot marigolds (calendula) are easy to grow, require little maintenance and bring colour to the garden. Not only are the flowers edible, they also act as a natural insect repellent, avoiding the need for pesticide sprays. To dry the flowers, remove the petals from the flower heads and spread out on a baking sheet, then leave overnight until dried and store in an airtight container.

Couscous makes a great base for stuffings as it takes on the flavours of stronger ingredients and adds substance. Here, it is mixed with harissa, which also doubles up as the flavouring of the sauce. Use large mushrooms with a slightly raised edge, which act like a bowl to hold the stuffing.

Roasted Mushrooms with Couscous Crust

Serves: 4   *Preparation time:* 15 minutes, plus making the stock
Cooking time: 35 minutes

75g/2½oz/heaped ⅓ cup couscous
hot Vegetable Stock (see page 14), to cover
3 tbsp olive oil, plus extra for drizzling
1 onion, finely chopped
2 large garlic cloves, finely chopped
1 tbsp harissa paste
1 tsp smoked mild paprika
1 large handful of flat-leaf parsley
   leaves, chopped
1 large handful of oregano leaves, chopped

4 large portobello or field mushrooms,
   stalks discarded
125g/4½oz rindless goats' cheese, crumbled
sea salt and freshly ground black pepper
mixed salad leaves, to serve

HARISSA MAYO
1 heaped tsp harissa
6 tbsp mayonnaise
juice of ½ lemon

1. Preheat the oven to 190°C/375°F/Gas 5. Put the couscous in a heatproof bowl and pour over enough hot stock to just cover. Stir, cover with a plate to keep in the heat and leave for 5 minutes, or until the stock is absorbed. Fluff up the couscous with a fork to separate the grains.

2. Meanwhile, heat half the oil in a large frying pan over a medium heat. Add the onion and fry for 8 minutes until softened but not coloured. Add the garlic and cook for another minute. Add the harissa, paprika, cooked couscous and half the herbs, season with salt and pepper and stir until combined.

3. Brush the top (not the gills) and edges of each mushroom with the remaining oil and put them in a small roasting tin to keep them upright. Spoon the couscous mixture in a pile on top, pressing it down slightly, then pour in 1 tablespoon water, cover with foil and roast for 15 minutes until the mushrooms have softened. Remove the foil, scatter the goats' cheese over the top of each one, drizzle with a little oil and return to the oven for another 10 minutes until the cheese has melted slightly.

4. Meanwhile, mix together all the ingredients for the harissa mayo with 1–2 tablespoons warm water and salt and pepper. Serve the mushrooms, sprinkled with the remaining herbs, with the harissa mayo and salad.

To dry robust herbs, such as rosemary, oregano, sage and thyme, put a single layer between two sheets of kitchen paper and microwave for 1–3 minutes.

This stir-fried rice dish is perfect for a weekday dinner. You could cook the rice the day before, but do reheat it thoroughly. You don't have to add the cashews, but I like their crunch in contrast to the softness of the rice.

Thai Rice with Spiced Cashews

Serves: 4   **Preparation time:** 20 minutes, plus cooling
Cooking time: 20 minutes

400g/14oz/2 cups Thai jasmine rice
3 tbsp sunflower oil
4 large spring onions, sliced, green and white
    parts kept separate
2 pak choi, white parts thinly sliced and green
    leaves thickly sliced
2 lemongrass stalks, outer leaves removed
    and finely chopped
1 red chilli, finely chopped
4cm/1½in piece of root ginger, finely chopped
4 garlic cloves, finely chopped

3 tbsp light soy sauce
juice of ½ lime
1 tsp sugar
1 small handful of basil leaves,
    preferably Thai, to serve

SPICED CASHEWS
100g/3½oz/⅔ cup cashew nuts
2 tsp Thai 7-spice
2 tsp soy sauce

1. Put the rice in a medium saucepan and pour in enough cold water to cover by 1cm/½in. Bring to the boil, then turn the heat down to its lowest setting and cover with a lid. Simmer for about 12 minutes, or until the water has been absorbed and the rice is tender. Turn off the heat and leave the rice to stand, still covered, for 5 minutes. Spread out the rice on a large plate and leave to cool.

2. Meanwhile, preheat the oven to 160°C/315°F/Gas 3. Put the cashews on a baking sheet and toast for 12 minutes, turning halfway. Mix together the 7-spice and soy sauce in a bowl. Add the toasted cashews and stir until coated in the spice mix. Tip the nuts back onto the baking sheet and return to the oven for another 3 minutes until crisp. Remove and leave to one side.

3. Heat the oil in a wok over a high heat. Add the white part of the spring onion and pak choi and stir-fry for 2 minutes, then add the lemongrass, chilli, green part of the pak choi, ginger and garlic and stir-fry for another 1 minute. Add the cooked, cooled rice and stir-fry for 3 minutes, or until piping hot. Mix together the soy sauce, lime juice and sugar until the sugar dissolves, then pour into the wok. Toss until combined and spoon onto plates. Scatter over the green part of the spring onion, the basil and the spiced cashew nuts.

If you have a large bag of nuts that you know won't be eaten right away, freeze them in zip-lock bags. There's no need to defrost them before use.

Thai 7-spice is also used in Crispy Thai-spiced Tofu (see page 43).

This risotto came about when I had just a handful of homegrown broad beans left – not enough to serve on their own. Broad beans are perfect with blue cheese, especially a creamy Dolcelatte, and there's no need for the usual addition, Parmesan, as this dish is plenty cheesy enough.

Last-of-the-Beans Risotto

Serves: 4 **Preparation time:** *10 minutes, plus making the stock and 10 minutes standing* **Cooking time:** *25 minutes*

250g/9oz/2 cups shelled fresh or frozen broad beans
30g/1oz butter
1 tbsp olive oil
1 large leek, finely chopped
320g/11¼oz/1¾ cups risotto rice
100ml/3½fl oz/scant ½ cup dry white wine or extra vegetable stock

1.2l/40fl oz/4¾ cups hot Vegetable Stock (see page 14)
175g/6oz Dolcelatte, chopped into bite-sized chunks
1 tbsp chopped flat-leaf parsley leaves
sea salt and freshly ground black pepper

1. Cook the broad beans in a pan of boiling water for about 3 minutes until just tender. Drain and refresh under cold running water, then remove the beans from their tough outer shell and leave to one side. Discard the tough outer shells.

2. Meanwhile, heat the butter and oil in a large, heavy-based pan. When melted, add the leek and sauté gently for 6 minutes until tender. Stir in the rice, and when coated in the buttery leeks, pour in the wine, if using. Let the wine bubble away until the alcohol evaporates and then start to add the stock, a ladleful at a time, stirring constantly. Only add the next ladleful when the previous one has been absorbed by the rice, and continue until the rice is creamy with just a slight bite. The rice should be slightly soupy, not dry, and takes about 25 minutes to cook in total.

3. When the rice is cooked, season with pepper and stir in the broad beans and Dolcelatte. Cover with a lid and leave to stand for 10 minutes. Taste and add a little salt, if needed, before serving sprinkled with parsley.

Leftover risotto rice can be used for Arancini Eggs (see page 68). Stir in 3 tablespoons grated vegetarian Parmesan instead of the broad beans and Dolcelatte.

Pearl barley is such an underrated grain and is enormously versatile, lending a creaminess and slightly chewy texture to chunky soups and stews, and substance to salads and pilaffs. It also makes an economical alternative to risotto rice. Go for pearl rather than pot barley, which takes much longer to cook.

Barley, Squash and Wild Oregano Risotto

Serves: 4   **Preparation time:** *15 minutes, plus making the stock*
Cooking time: *50 minutes*

680g/1lb 8oz butternut squash, peeled, deseeded and cut into large bite-sized pieces
1 bulb garlic, cloves separated but not peeled
1 handful of wild oregano or marjoram
4 tbsp olive oil
40g/1½oz butter
1 large onion, finely chopped

1 long red chilli, finely chopped, not deseeded
300g/10½oz/heaped 1⅓ cups pearl barley, rinsed
200ml/7fl oz/scant 1 cup dry white wine or extra vegetable stock
800ml/28fl oz/scant 3½ cups hot Vegetable Stock (see page 14)
sea salt and freshly ground black pepper

1. Preheat the oven to 190°C/375°F/Gas 5. Toss the squash, garlic cloves and 3 sprigs of the oregano in half the oil in a large roasting tin and roast for 20 minutes until the garlic has softened. Remove the garlic and oregano, turn the squash and return to the oven for another 10–15 minutes until tender and golden in places. Meanwhile, peel and roughly chop the garlic and leave to one side.

2. Remove the leaves from the remaining oregano, reserving 1 teaspoon, and put the rest in a small blender with the remaining olive oil and blend to make a herb oil. Leave to one side.

3. While the squash is roasting, melt the butter in a large, heavy-based saucepan over a medium heat. Add the onion and three-quarters of the chilli and sauté covered, for 8 minutes, until softened but not coloured. Add the barley and cook for 2 minutes, stirring to coat the grains in the buttery onions, and then pour in the wine, if using. Let the wine bubble away until absorbed by the grains, then stir in the hot vegetable stock all at once. Stir well until combined and simmer over a medium-low heat, part-covered, for 30–40 minutes until the grains are tender but still retain a slight bite.

4. Season with salt and pepper and stir in the herb oil, roasted squash and roasted garlic. Add a splash more stock or water, as you don't want the risotto to be too dry. Serve seasoned with extra pepper and sprinkled with the reserved oregano and chilli.

You'll be able to smell *wild* *oregano* before you spot it. This aromatic fresh herb loves grassy, chalky soil. The slightly downy leaves have pink or white flower heads, which are also edible. Oregano comes from the same family as marjoram and so I use these herbs interchangeably in cooking. In fact, you may be able to find wild marjoram in similar places, too.

Polenta

The beauty of polenta, the golden-yellow ground corn (maize), is that it's versatile and a great carrier of flavours – and it's cheap. Polenta is not just a staple in Northern Italy, where it's principally a winter food served as a type of savoury porridge with stews, it's also popular in the southern states of the US, where it's grown to make grits and cornbread. It makes a welcome alternative to carbs such as rice, pasta, bread and potatoes, and may come ground or in slabs for frying or grilling. Do bear in mind that the coarser the grain, the longer it takes to cook and the stronger your arm will have to be for all the stirring! Instant polenta cuts the cooking time to about 5–10 minutes. Use polenta as an alternative to mash, to make a crust for a tart, fried in cubes for croûtons, as crumbs for coating croquettes or in baking. For a flavour boost, add butter, cheese, herbs or chilli.

Grilled wedges of polenta with their soft, yielding interior and crisp, golden crust make an excellent alternative to toasted bread. Flavoured simply with Parmesan and chilli, the bruschetta go well served with the Moroccan Slow-Cooked Vegetables on page 159. Try experimenting with different flavourings, such as black olives, herbs, spices, sundried tomatoes, chargrilled aubergines or artichokes. Polenta freezes well – just prepare it up to the point it is cut into triangles, then freeze in individual pieces on a baking sheet. When frozen, transfer the polenta to a zip-lock bag for storing, then simply defrost and grill when ready to eat.

Polenta Bruschetta

Serves: *4–6*   **Preparation time:** *10 minutes, plus 30 minutes chilling*
Cooking time: *20 minutes*

175g/6oz/scant 1¼ cups instant polenta
40g/1½oz butter, diced
50g/1¾oz vegetarian Parmesan cheese,
   finely grated
1 tsp dried chilli flakes

1 tsp sea salt
olive oil, for brushing
1 recipe quantity Moroccan Slow-Cooked
   Vegetables (see page 159), to serve

1. Heat 850ml/29fl oz/scant 3½ cups water in a saucepan over a medium-low heat and when warm gradually stir in the polenta. Bring to the boil, then turn the heat down to low and simmer, stirring, for 10 minutes until thick and smooth; take care as it can splatter. Remove the pan from the heat and stir in the butter, Parmesan, chilli flakes and salt.

2. Lightly grease a large baking tray and spread the polenta into an even layer about 2cm/¾in thick, then leave to cool and set in the fridge. This will take about 30 minutes.

3. Preheat the grill to high (or you could use a ridged griddle pan). Cut the set polenta into 4 squares, then each one diagonally into a triangle. Brush one side of the polenta with oil and grill for 3–4 minutes until crisp and golden on the outside. Brush the top of the polenta with more oil, turn it over and grill for another 3–4 minutes. Serve with the Moroccan Slow-Cooked Vegetables.

Pictured on page 85.

Cheesy Chilli Cornbread

Preheat the oven to 190°C/375°F/Gas 5 and **butter** a 900g/2lb loaf tin. Mix together **165g/5¾oz/ heaped 1 cup instant polenta**, **75g/2½oz/scant ⅔ cup plain flour**, **2 tsp baking powder**, **½ tsp bicarbonate of soda**, **1 tsp sea salt**, **1 tsp English mustard powder**, **1 deseeded and chopped red chilli** and **75g/2½oz mature Cheddar cheese, grated**, in a large mixing bowl. Melt **60g/2¼oz butter** and combine with **2 large beaten eggs**, **200ml/7fl oz/scant 1 cup buttermilk** and **3 tablespoons milk**. Add the wet ingredients to the dry ingredients and pour into the prepared tin. Bake for 35–40 minutes, or until golden and a skewer inserted into the middle comes out clean.

Soft Polenta

Pour **500ml/17fl oz/2 cups Vegetable Stock** (see page 14) and **170ml/5½fl oz/⅔ cup milk** into a saucepan and bring to the boil. Add **165g/5¾oz/heaped 1 cup instant polenta** in a steady stream, stirring continuously, season and cook for 5 minutes until it is the consistency of soft mashed potato.

Polenta Tart Crust

Follow the ingredients and method for **Polenta Bruschetta**, opposite. After making, let it cool for about 5 minutes until it starts to firm up slightly. Spoon the polenta into a 25cm/10in loose-bottomed tart tin that has been greased with **olive oil**. Spread the polenta evenly over the bottom and up the sides to a thickness of about 5mm/¼in; there will be some left over, which can be used to patch up any cracks that appear. Preheat the oven to 190°C/350°F/Gas 5 and bake for 30 minutes, or until firm and crisp. Fill the polenta case with the filling of your choice.

Chapter 4
Bag of Nuts (and Seeds)

Delicious as a snack, nuts also make a valuable, nutritious and
sustaining base to a meal, whether it be a light and summery
Pecan, Pear and Nasturtium Salad, warming autumn
Chestnut and Mushroom Pie, a twist on the classic Italian
dumplings in the form of Semolina and Nut Milk Gnocchi,
or festive-inspired Roasted Onions with Nut Stuffing.
Similarly, the unassuming seed is transformed into a creamy,
spiced Tahini and Squash Dip, Sesame and Nori Cakes
or delicious puff-pastry Pumpkin Seed Rolls.

A jar of tahini is surprisingly versatile: hummus wouldn't be hummus without it, and a spoonful stirred into a miso stock makes a rich broth. I like to add a little to a soy-ginger dressing or use it as a healthier alternative to butter. Here, the sesame seed paste is turned into a moreish butternut squash dip, served with spicy flatbread crisps.

Tahini and Squash Dip

Serves: *6*   **Preparation time:** *15 minutes, plus making the yogurt and cooling*
Cooking time: *45 minutes*

1kg/2lb 4oz butternut squash, peeled,
    deseeded and cut into bite-sized chunks
3 tbsp olive oil, plus extra for brushing
1 tsp ground allspice
125ml/4fl oz/½ cup Wholemilk Yogurt
    (see page 16) or Greek yogurt
4 heaped tbsp light tahini paste
juice of 1 lemon
2 garlic cloves, crushed

2 tsp pomegranate molasses (optional)
1 tbsp sesame seeds, toasted (see page 18)
1 small handful of coriander leaves, chopped
sea salt and freshly ground black pepper

FLATBREAD CRISPS
6 round flatbreads
2 tbsp Dukka (see page 109)

1. Preheat the oven to 180°F/350°F/Gas 4. Put the squash in a large bowl and add the oil and allspice. Season well with salt and pepper and turn the squash with your hands until coated in the seasoned oil. Tip the squash onto a large baking sheet (or you may need two) and spread it out into an even layer. Roast for 45 minutes, turning once, or until tender and slightly golden on the edges. Leave to cool.

2. While the squash is roasting, use the heat of the oven to make the flatbread crisps. Brush one of the flatbreads with a little oil and put it in the oven with the roasting squash for 4–5 minutes, or until light golden and crisp; keep an eye on it, as it burns easily. Remove from the oven, brush with more oil and sprinkle over 1 teaspoon of the dukka, then repeat until you have prepared all 6 flatbreads. Pile on top of one another and leave to one side.

3. Put the roasted, cooled squash in a large bowl and add the yogurt, tahini, lemon juice, garlic and half the pomegranate molasses, if using, then mash with a potato masher to a coarse paste. You can do this in a food processor if you prefer a smoother dip. Season with salt and pepper. Drizzle the remaining pomegranate molasses over the top and sprinkle with the sesame seeds and coriander. Serve with the flatbread crisps.

Serve with Aubergine Meze (see page 158).

Keep flatbreads fresh by storing them in the freezer, then reheat under the grill or in a toaster from frozen when you need them.

Cut-and-come-again salad seeds are widely available and easy to grow, so it's feasible to have a constant supply of mixed leaves throughout the summer months – and even into the winter in a sheltered spot. Look for a seed mix that gives you a range of colours and textures, then simply harvest the leaves regularly to encourage new growth.

If I'm going to be using chopped walnuts in a recipe, I prefer to buy walnut pieces — not only do they save me the bother of chopping them, they are also much cheaper than the whole or halved equivalents. I steer clear of turning the oven on just to roast a small amount of nuts, so it makes sense to plan ahead, if you can, and utilize the oven for more than one dish.

Toasted Walnut Salad

Serves: 4   *Preparation time:* 10 minutes   *Cooking time:* 4 minutes

1 head of broccoli, large stalk removed,
   cut into small florets
3 handfuls of oakleaf or other red salad
   leaves, torn into large pieces
235g/8½oz/1⅓ cups drained tinned green
   lentils or cooked dried green lentils
   (see page 9)
½ red onion, diced
2 cooked beetroot, diced

1 handful of shredded red cabbage
2 handfuls of walnut pieces, toasted
   (see page 18)

DRESSING
4 tbsp extra virgin olive oil
2 tbsp balsamic vinegar, plus extra if needed
1 tsp clear honey
sea salt and freshly ground black pepper

1. Cook the broccoli in a pan of boiling salted water for 4 minutes until only just tender. Refresh under cold running water and leave to drain and cool.

2. Mix together the ingredients for the dressing — adding more balsamic vinegar if you like a sharper dressing — and season with salt and pepper.

3. Put the salad leaves on a large serving plate and scatter over the lentils, red onion, beetroot, red cabbage and cooked broccoli. Spoon the dressing over and toss lightly until combined, adding more salt and pepper if necessary. Scatter the walnuts over just before serving.

Serve with the Pumpkin Seed Rolls (see page 97).

Don't throw the broccoli stalk away; instead cut it into thin sticks and combine with strips of carrot and cabbage. Coat the vegetables in a mustardy mayonnaise dressing for an excellent twist on coleslaw.

The secret to the success of this vibrant salad is the combination of texture, colour and flavour. The sweet caramelized pears are perfect with the salty sharpness of the blue cheese, the peppery freshness of the leaves and the crunch of the toasted pecans. You can, of course, vary the combination to suit but do keep in mind the blend of salty, sweet, soft and crunch.

Pecan, Pear and Nasturtium Salad

Serves: 4   *Preparation time:* 15 minutes   *Cooking time:* 5 minutes

1 tbsp butter

2 slightly under-ripe pears, peeled, cored and each cut into 8 wedges

1 tsp ground ginger

1 tbsp clear honey

140g/5oz watercress

1 handful of nasturtium leaves and flowers

1 small red onion, thinly sliced

2 cooked beetroot, diced

2 handfuls of pecan halves, toasted (see page 18)

100g/3½oz crumbly blue cheese of choice

DRESSING

3 tbsp extra virgin olive oil

1 tbsp white wine vinegar

1 tsp Dijon mustard

sea salt and freshly ground black pepper

1. Melt the butter in a large, non-stick frying pan and cook the pears over a medium heat for 4 minutes, turning once, until softened. Stir in the ginger and honey, turn the pears to coat them in the syrupy mixture and cook for another minute.

2. Meanwhile, make the dressing. Whisk together the olive oil, vinegar and mustard and season with salt and pepper.

3. Divide the watercress and nasturtium leaves onto four serving plates. Top with the red onion and beetroot and drizzle the dressing over. Turn gently to coat the salad in the dressing, then top with the pecans, blue cheese, pears and nasturtium flowers before serving.

Not only do they look extremely attractive in the garden with their cheery-coloured petals, nasturtiums have both **edible** *leaves and edible flowers*. They are easy and undemanding plants to grow. The leaves have a peppery heat, while the flowers taste spicy and slightly sweet. They are both great in salads, valued for their taste as well as their looks.

This Roman version of gnocchi is made with semolina instead of the usual potato, and is baked in the oven. Don't waste any remnants of dough – they will keep in the fridge for a day or so and can be rolled into balls (then breadcrumbed, or not) and shallow-fried until crisp. As an alternative to the aubergine sauce, you can layer the gnocchi in an ovenproof dish, cover with your favourite pasta sauce and mozzarella and bake in the oven.

Semolina and Nut Milk Gnocchi

Serves: 4   **Preparation time:** 10 minutes, plus overnight chilling
Cooking time: 30 minutes

2 tbsp butter, melted, plus extra for greasing
500ml/17fl oz/2 cups unsweetened almond or cashew nut milk
1 tsp sea salt
¼ tsp freshly ground black pepper
150g/5½oz/heaped 1 cup semolina

2 large eggs, lightly beaten
85g/3oz vegetarian Parmesan cheese, finely grated
1 recipe quantity Aubergine Meze (see page 158), to serve

1. Line a large baking sheet with baking parchment and grease with butter. Pour the nut milk into a medium-sized saucepan, stir in the salt and pepper and bring it almost to the boil over a medium heat. Gradually add the semolina, stirring constantly with a wooden spoon, then turn the heat down to low and cook the semolina for 5 minutes, stirring, until you have a very thick paste. It will start to come away from the sides of the pan and be difficult to stir, but keep going for the full cooking time.

2. Remove the pan from the heat and beat in the eggs, three-quarters of the Parmesan and half the butter. Spoon the mixture onto the prepared baking sheet and, using a spatula, spread it out into an even layer about 1cm/½in thick. Occasionally dunk the spatula into water to stop the mixture sticking. Cover with a sheet of greased baking parchment and leave to cool (ideally, put it in the fridge overnight to firm up).

3. Preheat the oven to 200°C/400°F/Gas 6 and line a baking sheet with baking parchment. Cut the semolina into 16 × 6cm/2½in rounds using a cutter and place on the prepared sheet. Brush the gnocchi with the remaining melted butter and sprinkle with the rest of the Parmesan. Bake for 25 minutes, or until slightly risen and golden. Serve with the Aubergine Meze (page 158).

Make double the quantity and freeze uncooked gnocchi on a lined baking sheet. When frozen, transfer to a zip-lock bag. Defrost before baking.

I like to keep blocks of puff pastry (cheaper than the ready-rolled sheets you can buy) in the freezer, as they make a quick and convenient base – or topping – for sweet or savoury pies, tarts and galettes. This is my vegetarian version of the ever-popular sausage roll.

Pumpkin Seed Rolls

Serves: *10*   **Preparation time:** *15 minutes, plus 30 minutes chilling*
Cooking time: *40 minutes*

2 tbsp olive oil
1 large onion, finely chopped
150g/5½ oz chestnut mushrooms, finely
   chopped
4 tbsp pumpkin seeds
60g/2¼oz/½ cup finely chopped
   sundried tomatoes
140g/5oz/2½ cups fresh breadcrumbs
2 tsp harissa

finely grated zest of 1 lemon
2 eggs
1 tbsp thyme leaves or 2 tsp dried thyme
plain flour, for dusting
400g/14oz block frozen puff pastry, defrosted
   and halved
1 tbsp sesame seeds
sea salt and freshly ground black pepper

1. To make the filling, heat the oil in a large frying pan over a medium heat. Add the onion and fry for 5 minutes until softened, then add the mushrooms and cook for another 5 minutes until tender. Stir in the pumpkin seeds and cook for 3 minutes, stirring occasionally, until they start to pop and smell toasted. Add the sundried tomatoes and leave to cool a little before transferring to a mini food processor and blitzing to a coarse paste.

2. Transfer the paste to a bowl and stir in the breadcrumbs, harissa, lemon zest, 1 of the eggs and the thyme. Season with salt and pepper, then stir well until combined. Leave to cool.

3. Beat the remaining egg in a bowl. Lightly dust a work surface with flour and roll out the pastry into 2 × 38 × 15cm (15 × 6in) sheets, about 5mm/¼in thick. Divide the filling mixture in half and spoon one half down the long side of each pastry sheet. Using your hands, shape the filling into 2 long sausages, pressing the mixture to encourage it to hold together. Brush the edges of the pastry sheets with the beaten egg. Fold the pastry over the filling and press the edges together to make 2 tight rolls. Trim the edges, crimp with a fork and cut each roll into 5 pieces. Using a small knife, make light diagonal cuts on top of each roll, then brush the tops with beaten egg.

4. Put the rolls on a flour-dusted, non-stick baking sheet and chill for 30 minutes. Preheat the oven to 220°C/425°F/Gas 7. Remove the baking sheet from the fridge, brush the rolls with more egg and sprinkle with sesame seeds. Bake for 20–25 minutes until risen and golden, then leave to cool slightly before serving.

Sundried tomatoes are also used in Pizzata (see page 119).

You could make use of any leftover pastry and the hot oven to make cheese straws.

Great as a starter or a light meal, these light, fluffy Chinese buns have a filling of hoisin cashews and mushrooms. Surplus uncooked buns can be frozen on a baking sheet, then transferred to a freezer bag.

Yum Cha Buns

Makes: *8 large buns*   **Preparation time:** *30 minutes, plus about 2 hours rising*
Cooking time: *15 minutes, or more if cooking in batches*

5g/⅛oz dried yeast
2 tsp sugar
200g/7oz/scant 1⅔ cups plain flour,
   plus extra for dusting
½ tsp salt
¾ tsp baking powder
1½ tbsp sunflower oil, plus extra for greasing

CASHEW FILLING
200g/7oz chestnut mushrooms, finely chopped
2.5cm/1in piece of root ginger, peeled and
   very finely chopped
3 tbsp hoisin sauce, plus extra to serve
3 spring onions, finely chopped
55g/2oz/⅓ cup toasted cashew nuts
   (see page 18), finely chopped
freshly ground black pepper

1. To make the dough, pour 135ml/4½fl oz/generous ½ cup tepid water into a small bowl and sprinkle over the yeast and sugar. Stir until the sugar dissolves, then leave for 10 minutes until frothy. Sift the flour, salt and baking powder into a large mixing bowl, stir and make a well in the centre. Pour the yeast mixture and 1½ teaspoons of the oil into the well and gradually mix in the flour to form a soft ball of dough. Turn out onto a lightly floured work surface and knead for 10 minutes until you have a smooth and elastic ball of dough. Wipe the inside of the cleaned mixing bowl with a little oil. Add the dough, cover the bowl with cling film and leave in a warm place until doubled in size, about 2 hours.

2. Meanwhile, make the filling. Heat a wok over a high heat, add the remaining oil and stir-fry the mushrooms and ginger for 8 minutes, or until any liquid evaporates. Spoon the mixture into a bowl and stir in the hoisin, spring onions and cashews. Season with pepper, and leave to one side.

3. Turn the dough out onto a lightly floured surface. Divide into 8 balls and cover with a damp tea towel. Take a dough ball and press it into a round about 5mm/¼in thick, then put a heaped tablespoonful of the mushroom mixture in the centre of the dough and pull the edges up over the filling, pressing them together to seal. Put on a lightly floured surface and repeat with remaining balls and filling.

4. Put the buns in a tiered steamer, lined with baking parchment. Cover with a lid and steam for 15 minutes, or until risen and fluffy. (You can cook the buns in batches, if necessary.) Serve the buns warm with extra hoisin sauce for dipping.

Grow *rainbow chard*, and you will not only be rewarded with dazzling magenta, orange, red and yellow stalks topped with verdant leaves, but you can keep a steady supply throughout the summer and well into the winter months. Simply harvest the outer leaves to allow new growth. The small, young leaves can be eaten in salads, while more established leaves are good braised, steamed or stir-fried.

Here, the most simple of ingredients are turned into something special with very little effort. The baked onions are served simply with steamed rainbow chard, but they would also be delicious with a cauliflower purée made by boiling the florets in vegetable stock, then blending them with a little single cream and salt and pepper.

Roasted Onions with Nut Stuffing

Serves: 4   *Preparation time:* 10 minutes   *Cooking time:* 1 hour 15 minutes

4 onions, unpeeled
4 thick slices of country-style bread
4 tbsp olive oil
4 tsp balsamic vinegar
sea salt and freshly ground black pepper
steamed rainbow chard, to serve

NUT STUFFING
55g/2oz/heaped ⅓ cup blanched almonds,
**   toasted (see page 18)**
55g/2oz/scant ½ cup sunflower seeds,
**   toasted (see page 18)**
3 tbsp day-old breadcrumbs
finely grated zest of 1 lemon
4 tbsp chopped flat-leaf parsley leaves
2 tbsp chopped rosemary or sage leaves

1. Preheat the oven to 180°C/350°F/Gas 4. Trim the root end of each onion so it stands up and then slice a cross into the top, cutting about halfway down. Remove any loose skin from the onions, put each one on a slice of bread and transfer to a small baking tin. Spoon a quarter of the oil and the balsamic vinegar over the top of each onion and season with salt and pepper. Cover the dish with foil and bake for 60 minutes, or until the centre of the onions are tender when prodded with a skewer.

2. Meanwhile, make the stuffing. Coarsely grind the toasted almonds and sunflower seeds in a mini food processor. Tip them into a bowl and mix in the rest of the stuffing ingredients with the remaining oil, and season with salt and pepper.

3. Remove the onions from the oven. Take off the foil, carefully open up the onions slightly and divide the stuffing mixture among them, spooning it into the centre of each one. Return to the oven, uncovered, and roast for another 15 minutes until the stuffing has heated through and is slightly crisp on top. Serve the onions on their slice of cooked bread with the rainbow chard on the side.

Like tofu, tempeh is made from fermented soya beans, but it has a nuttier, coarser texture. You can buy tempeh chilled, but I tend to buy it frozen in large blocks so I can simply slice off the amount needed.

Tempeh with Peanut Sauce

Serves: 4   **Preparation time:** 15 minutes, plus at least 1 hour marinating
Cooking time: 25 minutes

2 tbsp dark soy sauce
1 tbsp clear honey
1 tbsp sunflower oil
1 tbsp toasted sesame oil
200g/7oz tempeh or tofu, drained, patted dry
    and cubed
250g/9oz medium egg noodles
chopped spring onions and coriander leaves,
    to serve

PEANUT SAUCE
75g/2½oz/½ cup peanut butter
2 tbsp rice wine vinegar
2 tbsp dark soy sauce
2 tbsp soft light brown sugar
1 tbsp tahini paste
½ tsp dried chilli flakes
2.5cm/1in piece of root ginger,
    peeled and chopped
1 tsp turmeric

1. Mix together the soy sauce, honey, sunflower oil and sesame oil in a shallow dish. Add the tempeh and turn to coat it in the marinade, then leave to marinate for 1 hour, or until ready to use – the longer the better.

2. Meanwhile, make the peanut sauce. Blend together all the ingredients with 4 tablespoons hot water until smooth, then leave to one side.

3. Preheat the oven to 190°C/350°F/Gas 5. Remove the tempeh from the marinade and spread it out on a large baking sheet. Roast for 25 minutes, turning once, until golden all over.

4. Meanwhile, cook the noodles following the pack instructions. Drain, reserving a little of the cooking water. Return the noodles to the pan and stir in the peanut sauce, adding as much of the reserved cooking water as needed to make a slightly runny sauce. Serve the peanut noodles topped with the tempeh, sprinkled with spring onions and coriander.

Tahini is also used in the Tahini and Squash Dip (see page 90).

Make double the quantity of peanut sauce and freeze for up to 3 months. Reheat from frozen with a splash of water, and use as a sauce, a dip or the base of a dressing.

This curry changes depending on what I have lying around in the kitchen. So you could also use a combination of red pepper, spinach and mushrooms, or root veg in the winter for a more substantial dish. Similarly, try making your own blends of spice mixes (see page 15); this one has a Sri Lankan feel and works well with coconut-based curries.

Sri Lankan Coconut Curry

Serves: 4   *Preparation time:* 15 minutes, plus making the spice mix
Cooking time: 25 minutes

1 large onion
4 garlic cloves
5cm/2in piece of root ginger, peeled and sliced
3 tbsp sunflower oil
2½ tbsp Curry Spice Mix (see page 15) or medium curry powder
400g/14fl oz/2 cups coconut milk
3 tomatoes, deseeded and chopped

1 tsp vegetable bouillon powder
1 cauliflower, cut into small florets
100g/3½oz fine green beans, cut into thirds
juice of 1 lime
1 tsp soft light brown sugar
3 handfuls of fresh coriander leaves and stalks, chopped
sea salt and freshly ground black pepper
2 tbsp toasted flaked almonds, to serve

1. Put the onion, garlic and ginger in a food processor and blend to a coarse paste. Heat the oil in a large, heavy-based saucepan over a medium-low heat, add the onion paste and fry for 5 minutes, stirring regularly, until softened.

2. Stir in 2 tablespoons of the spice mix, then add the coconut milk, tomatoes and 250ml/9fl oz/1 cup water and bring up to boiling point. Stir in the bouillon powder, turn the heat down slightly and simmer for 5 minutes.

3. Add the cauliflower and green beans and cook, part-covered, for 12 minutes until the vegetables are almost cooked. Stir in the lime juice, sugar, 2 handfuls of the coriander and the remaining spice mix. Season well and cook, part-covered, for another 3 minutes or until the vegetables are tender. Remove the lid if the sauce needs to thicken. Serve sprinkled with the almonds and the remaining coriander.

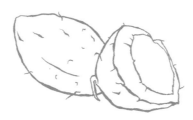

Tins of coconut milk are often cheaper in Asian grocers', or check out the 'world food' section in supermarkets.

Wild sweet chestnuts are delicious in this autumnal pie, with its crisp suet crust. If you are roasting them, make sure you cut a small slit in the skin first or they may explode in the oven – believe me, I speak from experience!

Chestnut and Mushroom Pie

Serves: *4–6*   **Preparation time:** *20 minutes, plus 30 minutes chilling*
Cooking time: *1 hour*

2 tbsp sunflower oil
3 leeks, chopped
2 carrots, diced (or you could use any leftover
    cooked root vegetables)
375g/13oz chestnut mushrooms, chopped
3 garlic cloves, finely chopped
200g/7oz cooked peeled chestnuts, chopped
1 heaped tbsp chopped sage leaves
1 heaped tbsp thyme leaves or
    2 tsp dried thyme
1 heaped tbsp plain flour
200ml/7fl oz/scant 1 cup light ale

200ml/7fl oz/scant 1 cup Vegetable Stock
    (see page 14)
1 egg, lightly beaten
sea salt and freshly ground black pepper

SUET PASTRY
250g/9oz/2 cups plain flour, plus extra
    for dusting
½ tsp baking powder
125g/4½oz/1 cup vegetable suet
½ tsp sea salt

1. Mix together the flour, baking powder, suet and salt in a large mixing bowl. Stir in 160ml/5¼fl oz/⅔ cup water and bring together to make a ball of dough. Wrap in cling film and chill for 30 minutes.

2. Meanwhile, make the pie filling. Heat the oil in a large, heavy-based pan over a medium heat. Add the leeks and carrots, turn the heat down slightly and cook, part-covered, for 6 minutes until the leeks are tender. Add the mushrooms and cook for another 4 minutes until tender. Stir in the garlic, chestnuts and herbs, then add the flour and cook, stirring, for 1 minute. Pour in the ale, stir, and gently boil, uncovered, for 5 minutes or until reduced by half. Add the stock and cook, part-covered, for 10 minutes. Remove the lid if the sauce is too thin. Season with salt and pepper.

3. Preheat the oven to 190°C/375°F/Gas 5. Tip the filling into a 25 × 29cm (10 × 11½in) pie dish. Roll out the pastry on a lightly floured work surface until 5mm/¼in thick. Cut a long 1cm/½in strip of pastry from the edge. Brush the rim of the pie dish with a little beaten egg, top with the pastry strip and brush with more egg. Top with the pastry lid, then press and crimp the edges. Brush the top with egg and prick the middle with a fork. Bake for 30 minutes until cooked and golden.

You can gather **sweet chestnuts** in the autumn. They're easier to harvest when they've dropped to the ground, but retrieve them early in the day before the squirrels get them! Cook the chestnuts in a pan of simmering water until the kernels are tender, then refresh in cold water and peel. Alternatively, roast them in the oven or cook in a special chestnut pan over a hob or open fire.

Sesame Seeds

Traditionally from Africa, slaves brought sesame seeds to America, yet these unassuming seeds are used in the cooking of a surprisingly diverse collection of countries located across the globe; their diminutive size does not appear to have held them back in any way. For example, in Europe sesame seeds are sprinkled over sweet and savoury pastries and breads before baking, while in the Middle East they are ground into the thick, creamy paste known as tahini. In Japan, gomashio – made by grinding sesame seeds with salt – is a popular seasoning, and distinctive toasted sesame oil is often sprinkled over Far Eastern dishes at the end of cooking. The seeds, which come in red, black, yellow and the more usual creamy white, have a high oil content so are best kept in an airtight container in the fridge or freezer to stop them turning rancid.

▶▶

The nutty flavour of sesame seeds is greatly enhanced by lightly toasting them in a dry frying pan until they are just golden. Here, the seeds are combined with toasted flakes of nori and folded into sticky sushi rice to make Japanese-style patties, and then topped with some mustardy greens, thin strips of omelette and a sprinkling of peppery radish sprouts.

Sesame and Nori Cakes

Serves: *4*   **Preparation time:** *15 minutes, plus 10 minutes standing*
Cooking time: *25 minutes*

375g/13oz/1¾ cups sushi rice, rinsed 3 times
2 nori sheets
3 tbsp sesame seeds
25g/1oz butter
6 eggs
2 heaped tbsp radish sprouts
sea salt and freshly ground black pepper

MUSTARD-SOY GREENS
1 sweetheart cabbage or 4 pak choi, sliced
2 tbsp English mustard
4 tbsp lemon juice
2 tbsp light soy sauce

1. Put the rice in a saucepan, cover with 500ml/17fl oz/2 cups water and add 1 teaspoon salt. Bring to the boil, then cover with a lid, turn the heat down to its lowest setting and simmer for 10–12 minutes until the water has been absorbed and the rice is tender and sticky. Remove from the heat and leave to stand for 10 minutes, covered, until cooled slightly.

2. Meanwhile, heat a large, non-stick, dry frying pan over a medium heat. Toast the nori sheets, one at a time, for 1½ minutes on each side, or until just crisp, then leave to cool. Add the sesame seeds to the pan and toast for 2 minutes until just golden.

3. Add the sesame seeds to the rice in the pan. Tear the nori sheets into small pieces and fold them into the rice in the pan with the sesame seeds, replace the lid and leave to one side while you steam the greens for 3 minutes until just tender. While the greens are cooking, mix together the mustard, lemon juice, soy sauce and 2 tablespoons water. Tip the cooked greens into a bowl, pour the mustard dressing over and turn until coated.

4. To make the omelettes, melt half the butter in the frying pan over a medium heat. Lightly beat 3 of the eggs in a bowl, season with salt and pepper and pour into the frying pan. Turn the heat down slightly and swirl the pan so the egg covers the base and cook until just firm. Roll up the omelette, tip it onto a plate and repeat to make a second one. Cut each omelette into thin strips crossways. With wet hands, form the sushi rice mixture into 4 round patties. Spoon the dressed greens on top in a pile and top with the omelette strips and radish sprouts.

Pictured on page 107.

Dukka

This Egyptian mix of toasted nuts, seeds and spices is addictively moreish. Toast **3 tbsp coriander seeds**, **1 tbsp cumin seeds** and **3 tbsp each of sesame seeds**, **sunflower seeds** and **pumpkin seeds** in a large, dry frying pan for 2–3 minutes, shaking the pan occasionally until they smell toasted and are lightly coloured. Remove from the pan and leave to cool. Toast **55g/2oz/⅓ cup blanched almonds** and **30g/1oz/scant ¼ cup hazelnuts** in the same pan for 5 minutes, then leave to cool. Tip the toasted nuts, seeds and spices into a mini grinder and grind to a coarse crumbly mixture. Transfer to a bowl, stir in **½ tsp dried chilli flakes** and season well with **salt** and **pepper**.

Tamari Nuts and Seeds

Great for snacking on or sprinkled over stir-fries and rice dishes, tamari-coated nuts and seeds don't take long to make. Preheat the oven to 170°C/325°F/Gas 3. Put **2 handfuls of mixed nuts**, such as almonds, cashews and peanuts, in a bowl. Add **2 handfuls of mixed seeds**, including sesame, sunflower and pumpkin, then stir in **2–3 tbsp tamari** or **soy sauce** until everything is coated. Tip onto a large baking sheet (or you may need two) and spread out in an even layer. Roast for 10–12 minutes, turning regularly, until they smell toasted. Keep an eye on them, as they burn easily. Tip into a bowl, leave to cool and store in an airtight container.

Sesame, Orange and Dandelion Salad

Toast **2 tbsp sesame seeds** in a dry frying pan until light golden. Wash **2 handfuls of young dandelion leaves**, drain well and put on a serving plate with **2 handfuls of watercress**. Slice **1 peeled orange** into rounds and put on top of the salad leaves. Mix together **2 tbsp extra virgin olive oil** with **1 tsp clear honey** and **1 tbsp lemon juice**, season with **salt** and **pepper** and spoon the dressing over the salad.

Chapter 5
Carton of Eggs

The perfect complete, nutritious food encased in a convenient, individual package, the egg is a marvel of versatility and for very little expense. Whether scrambled, boiled, fried, poached or baked, used to thicken sauces, to bind fritters or to add a golden glaze to pastry-topped pies, eggs are a must in my kitchen. Look out for Twice-Baked Cheese Soufflés, Easter Egg Pies, Tunisian Eggs with Herb Yogurt and last, but by no means least, a Rainbow Chard and Parmesan Tortino in this chapter.

This is based on the iconic Greek soup avgolemono, but is made with vegetable stock and added courgettes to form a light first course or a summery lunch. You could make it more substantial by upping the vegetables, perhaps including asparagus tips, fresh peas or broad beans when they are in season. I've used vermicelli pasta, but you could also try orzo, rice or even thin egg noodles.

Greek Egg and Lemon Soup

Serves: *4*　**Preparation time:** *10 minutes, plus making the stock*
Cooking time: *3 minutes*

1.2l/40fl oz/4¾ cups Vegetable Stock
　(see page 14)
115g/4oz/1 cup dried vermicelli pasta
1 large or 2 small courgettes, diced
juice and finely grated zest of 1 lemon

2 tsp cornflour
2 large eggs
sea salt and freshly ground black pepper
fennel fronds, to serve

1. Bring the stock to the boil in a large saucepan. Add the vermicelli and courgette and cook for 3 minutes until both are tender. Season with salt and pepper.

2. Meanwhile, put the lemon juice and zest in a mixing bowl and stir in the cornflour until dissolved, then whisk in the eggs until combined.

3. Remove the pan from the heat, add a spoonful of the hot stock to the egg mixture and whisk until combined. Pour the egg mixture into the pan, stirring continuously for a couple of minutes until the soup thickens slightly. Serve sprinkled with wild fennel fronds and seasoned with extra pepper.

Place an egg in a bowl of cold water – if it sinks horizontally, it's very fresh. If it tips up slightly, it could be up to 2 weeks old. If it floats, throw it away.

The fronds of *wild fennel* are prolific throughout the summer months, especially on wasteground and coastal areas. Like cultivated Florence fennel, the fronds have a sweet aniseed flavour, but the wild variety doesn't produce a bulb. Use the fronds as a flavourful herb and the thin stems sliced into salads. Clusters of yellow flowers produce seeds that can be harvested and dried in autumn.

Spring onions are easy to grow from seed in pots in a sunny spot or in fertilized soil with good drainage. They are quick-growing; sow regularly from spring to late summer to ensure a steady supply. I'm also a fan of milder red spring onions. Thin out young shoots to prevent overcrowding, and use in salads in the same way as chives or use in stir-fries, pilaffs, tortillas or stirred into mash.

This Mexican dish is a great way of using up slightly stale tortillas (which in my house have a tendency to linger in the back of the bread bin). I can't claim that my version of this classic dish is authentic, as I mix the tomato salsa into the scrambled eggs rather than into the tortillas, and then serve the scramble on top of the crisp, fried tortillas, yet it still goes down well with the family.

Chilaquiles

Serves: 4   *Preparation time:* 15 minutes   *Cooking time:* 17 minutes

6 corn tortillas
sunflower oil, for frying
4 vine-ripened tomatoes, deseeded and diced
6 spring onions, thinly sliced
1 red chilli, deseeded and chopped
1 large handful of coriander leaves, chopped
30g/1oz butter

10 eggs, lightly beaten
good splash of chilli sauce
sea salt and freshly ground black pepper

TO SERVE
bottled jalapeños, chopped
feta or other soft cheese, crumbled

1. Stack the tortillas on top of one another and cut them into 12 wedges. Pour a good layer of oil into a large frying pan and heat over a medium heat. Fry the tortilla wedges in four batches for about 1 minute on each side until light golden and crisp, then drain on kitchen paper and leave to one side.

2. Mix together the tomatoes, spring onions, chilli and half the coriander. Pour all but 1 tablespoon of the oil out of the pan, turn the heat down to medium-low and add the butter. When the butter has melted, add the tomato salsa and cook, stirring, for 3 minutes until softened.

3. Season the eggs with salt and pepper and stir in the chilli sauce. Add to the pan and cook the eggs over a low heat, turning the mixture gently until everything is combined and scrambled to a soft but cooked consistency.

4. Divide the tortilla wedges onto four serving plates and top with the scrambled egg mixture and the remaining coriander. Scatter over the jalapeños and feta before serving.

You can't beat the flavour of tomatoes ripened on the vine, but if you're faced with hard tomatoes store them in a paper bag with a ripe banana or an apple to encourage ripening; the same technique works with avocados, too.

This is a great throw-together dish, made predominantly from staple ingredients. There are many North African variations of Tunisian Eggs, which are all based on the same idea but vary slightly in their use of spicing and choice of herbs. I also like to crumble Homemade Paneer (see page 17) or other soft, crumbly cheese over the top just before serving.

Tunisian Eggs with Herb Yogurt

Serves: *4*　**Preparation time:** *15 minutes*　**Cooking time:** *30 minutes*

3 tbsp olive oil
1 large onion, finely chopped
3 garlic cloves, finely chopped
1 large red pepper, deseeded and chopped
2 tsp ground coriander
1 tsp ground cumin
1 tsp hot smoked paprika
½ tsp dried chilli flakes
2 tsp thyme leaves or 1 tsp dried thyme
400g/14oz tinned chopped tomatoes
1 tsp soft light brown sugar
4 large eggs

sea salt and freshly ground black pepper
crusty bread, to serve

HERB YOGURT
150ml/5fl oz/scant ⅔ cup Wholemilk Yogurt
   (see page 16) or Greek yogurt
1 garlic clove, crushed
4 heaped tbsp chopped coriander leaves
2 tbsp chopped mint leaves, plus extra
   to serve
1 small handful of toasted chopped walnuts
¼ tsp sumac (optional)

1. Heat the oil in a large, deep frying pan over a medium heat. Add the onion and fry for 6 minutes until softened but not coloured. Add the garlic and red pepper and cook for another 3 minutes, turning the heat down slightly if things start to brown. Stir in the spices and thyme followed by the tomatoes and sugar, then bring to the boil.

2. Turn the heat down to low and simmer, part-covered, for 10 minutes until reduced and thickened. Season with salt and pepper and make four evenly spaced dips in the sauce. Crack the eggs into the dips, cover with a lid and cook gently for 8 minutes, or until the egg whites are set but the yolks are still a little runny.

3. While the eggs are cooking, mix together the yogurt, garlic, coriander and mint in a bowl. Season with salt and pepper and scatter over the walnuts and sumac, if using. Sprinkle the eggs with extra mint and serve with the herb yogurt and crusty bread.

Preparing baked eggs is pretty straightforward, and quantities can readily be increased or decreased depending on how many you're feeding. This version is topped with a curry-spiced cream and gives a simple twist on the classic eggs Florentine with spinach, cream and a sprinkling of cheese. I've made the most of some foraged wild field mushrooms, though you could also use puffballs or, if you're lucky enough to find them, ceps.

Spiced Baked Eggs

Serves: *4*   **Preparation time:** *10 minutes*   **Cooking time:** *25 minutes*

30g/1oz butter, plus extra for greasing
2 tsp olive oil
250g/9oz field mushrooms or mushrooms of
   choice, finely chopped
5 large handfuls of Swiss chard, tough stalks
   removed, leaves shredded

4 large eggs
125ml/4fl oz/½ cup double cream
1 tbsp mild curry powder
sea salt and freshly ground black pepper
toasted bread, to serve

1. Preheat the oven to 190°C/375°F/Gas 5 and lightly butter four deep ramekin dishes. Heat the butter and oil in a large frying pan over a medium heat. Add the mushrooms and fry for 4 minutes until any liquid has evaporated and they start to turn crisp. Add the chard and cook for another 3–4 minutes until wilted and tender.

2. Divide the mushroom mixture into the prepared ramekins, then crack an egg into each one. Mix together the cream and curry powder, season with salt and pepper and spoon over the eggs so they are completely covered.

3. Put the ramekins in a deep baking dish and pour in enough just-boiled water to come three-quarters of the way up the sides. This will help the eggs to cook evenly. Carefully transfer the dish to the oven and cook for 16–18 minutes until the whites of the eggs are just set but the yolks remain runny (you can cook them for slightly longer if you prefer a set egg). Season with more pepper and serve with toasted bread.

This is a hybrid of my children's two favourite things – pizza and frittata – and makes a simple midweek meal when served with a mixed salad. Feel free to add your own favourite toppings or whatever you have to hand; this is a great way to use up leftover cheese, vegetables, olives, capers or anything else you choose. You need a heavy-based 22cm/8½in non-stick pan with an ovenproof handle.

Pizzata

Serves: *4* **Preparation time:** *15 minutes* **Cooking time:** *20 minutes*

3 Charlotte potatoes, peeled and quartered
2 tbsp olive oil
1 large onion, chopped
4 sundried tomatoes, chopped
8 eggs, lightly beaten
125g/4½oz drained mozzarella cheese, patted dry and torn into pieces

1 long red chilli, deseeded and chopped (optional)
6 tsp basil pesto
1 handful of small basil leaves
sea salt and freshly ground black pepper

1. Cook the potatoes in boiling salted water for 10 minutes, or until tender. Drain and leave to cool slightly, then dice.

2. Meanwhile, heat the oil in a large, deep, non-stick ovenproof frying pan over a medium heat. Add the onion and fry for 8 minutes until softened but not coloured. Stir in the cooked potatoes and sundried tomatoes and spread over the base of the pan in an even layer.

3. Preheat the grill to medium. Season the eggs with salt and pepper, then pour them into the pan over the onion mixture. Turn the heat down to medium-low and cook the eggs gently, without stirring, for 8 minutes, or until the base is set and light golden. Scatter the mozzarella and chilli, if using, over the top and dot with spoonfuls of the pesto. Grill for 2–3 minutes until the mozzarella has just melted. Serve sprinkled with the basil and cut into wedges.

Sundried tomatoes are also used in Pumpkin Seed Rolls (see page 97).

If your frying pan has lost its non-stick coating, you can temper it for a new lease of life. First add a little oil and rub it all over the pan with a sheet of kitchen paper. Heat the pan over a high heat until the oil starts to smoke, then remove the pan from the heat. Using a large crumpled piece of kitchen paper, wipe the base of the pan, taking care not to burn yourself. Leave the pan to cool, and it is ready to use.

These are based on the Greek Easter pie, which is filled with foraged wild greens, and traditionally celebrates the arrival of spring. For a change, I've hidden an egg in the centre of each pie. You could use a deep muffin tin for the pies instead of pudding basins.

Easter Egg Pies

Serves: 4   *Preparation time:* 20 minutes   *Cooking time:* 55 minutes

60g/2¼oz butter, melted
5 small eggs
2 tbsp olive oil
1 large onion, finely chopped
2 garlic cloves, finely chopped
260g/9¼oz greens, such as nettles, rocket and
    chard, stalks removed, leaves shredded

250g/9oz/2 cups curd cheese
4 tsp thyme leaves or 2 tsp dried thyme
½ tsp freshly grated nutmeg
8 sheets of filo pastry, 30 × 26cm/12 × 10½in
sea salt and freshly ground black pepper

1. Preheat the oven to 190°C/375°F/Gas 5 and brush four deep metal pudding basins (about 200ml/7fl oz/ scant 1 cup) with some of the melted butter. Hard-boil 4 of the eggs, then refresh under cold running water, peel and leave to one side. Meanwhile, heat the oil in a large frying pan over a medium heat. Add the onion and fry for 8 minutes until softened and starting to colour. Stir in the garlic and cook for another 2 minutes, stirring regularly.

2. If using nettles, wash them well and cook in a pan with no extra water for 4 minutes to neutralize the sting. Drain well, pat dry and tip into a large bowl with the onion mixture. Stir in the remaining mixed greens, curd cheese, thyme and nutmeg. Lightly beat the remaining egg and add to the bowl, season well with salt and pepper and stir until combined.

3. Lay out 1 sheet of the filo, brush half with butter and fold in half to cover the butter-coated part. Carefully press the filo into one of the prepared basins, leaving the excess pastry overhanging. Repeat with a second sheet of filo, then put it across the first sheet and press it into the basin to make a pastry case, again leaving an overhang.

4. Put a large tablespoonful of the greens mixture in the base of the pastry-lined basin and put a peeled hard-boiled egg upright in it. Spoon the greens mixture around and on top of the egg, pressing down with your fingers and filling the basin to the brim. Brush the overhanging pastry with more melted butter and fold it over the filling, scrunching to seal the top. Brush with more butter, then repeat to make 4 pies. Put the pies on a baking sheet and bake for 30–40 minutes until golden and crisp. Leave to cool slightly in the basins, then carefully turn out. If the pastry shells are a little soft, return the pies to the oven for another 5 minutes to crisp up.

Forage for *nettles* in spring, when the leaves are young and tender. Wearing thick gloves and using scissors, gather the youngest leaves and, as the season progresses, only pick the tips – the older leaves can be bitter. Gather nettles away from roads, wash well before cooking and enjoy this herby, nutritious leaf – a good source of iron, vitamins A and C and a surprisingly generous amount of protein.

If you've always shied away from making soufflés, I've found these fail-proof. They can be made the day before and reheated briefly before serving; they magically rise up when baked for the second time.

Twice-Baked Cheese Soufflés

Serves: 4   **Preparation time:** 15 minutes, plus 30 minutes infusing
Cooking time: 50 minutes

200ml/7fl oz/scant 1 cup milk
1 bay leaf
1 large garlic clove, halved
50g/1¾oz butter
40g/1½oz/⅓ cup plain flour
2 tsp Dijon mustard
140g/5oz/1½ cups grated mature
   Cheddar cheese

2 tbsp snipped chives, plus extra
   to serve
3 eggs, separated
4 tbsp double cream
crisp green salad, to serve

1. Heat the milk in a small saucepan with the bay leaf and garlic until warm, then turn off the heat and leave to infuse for 30 minutes. Remove the bay leaf and garlic from the milk and reheat until warm. Meanwhile, preheat the oven to 200°C/400°F/Gas 6 and heat a large baking sheet.

2. Melt the butter in a medium saucepan and use a little to grease four 200ml/7fl oz/scant 1 cup deep ramekins. Whisk the remaining melted butter with the flour over a medium heat and cook, stirring, for 1 minute.

3. Gradually stir the warm milk into the flour mixture. Bring to the boil, then turn the heat down to low and simmer for 5 minutes, stirring, until thick and smooth. Pour the soufflé mixture into a bowl and stir in the mustard, Cheddar and chives. Beat in the egg yolks, one at a time.

4. In a separate large bowl, whisk the egg whites until they form stiff peaks. Using a metal spoon, fold the egg whites into the cheese mixture in two batches, then spoon it into the prepared ramekins. Put the ramekins on the heated baking sheet and bake for 18–20 minutes until risen. Leave to cool, run a knife around the edge of the soufflés and turn them out. Chill until ready to serve.

5. Just before serving, heat the oven to 220°C/425°F/Gas 7. Put the soufflés on a baking sheet, then spoon 1 tablespoon of the cream over each one. Bake for 10–12 minutes until risen. Sprinkle the soufflés with the chives and serve with a green salad.

This has a Scandi feel, with the crisp, golden latkes topped with soft-boiled eggs and a mustard soured cream sauce. A sprinkling of wild fennel fronds adds the finishing touch. Freeze any leftover cooked and cooled latkes on a baking sheet in the freezer, then transfer to a zip-lock bag. Reheat from frozen in the oven until crisp and heated through.

Potato and Parsnip Latkes with Wild Fennel

Serves: 4   *Preparation time:* 20 minutes   *Cooking time:* 20 minutes

2 white potatoes, about 550g/1lb 4oz
2 parsnips, about 300g/10½oz
5 tbsp plain flour
1 tsp baking powder
1 tbsp fennel or caraway seeds
1 tsp sea salt
¼ tsp coarsely ground black pepper
2 eggs, lightly beaten
sunflower oil, for shallow-frying

TO SERVE
6 large eggs
125ml/4fl oz/½ cup soured cream
2 tsp English mustard
3 cooked beetroot, diced
a few wild fennel fronds (see page 113)

1. Coarsely grate the potatoes and parsnips using a box grater or a food processor; ideally you want long, thin strands. Transfer half the vegetables to a clean tea towel and wring out as much liquid as possible, then repeat with the remaining vegetables. Put in a bowl and stir in the flour, baking powder, fennel seeds, salt and pepper until combined. Add the beaten eggs and stir again.

2. Preheat the oven to 70°C/150°F/Gas ¼. Heat enough oil to cover the base of a large, non-stick frying pan over a medium heat. Take a small handful of the vegetable mixture, letting the eggy batter drain off a little, and put it into the pan. Flatten slightly with a spatula into a rough-edged 9cm/3½in round, then repeat so you have 3 latkes in the pan, and fry for 3 minutes on each side until golden and crisp. Transfer the latkes to a kitchen paper-lined baking sheet and keep warm in the oven while you cook the remaining latkes. The mixture will make 8 in total.

3. Put the eggs in a saucepan and cover with cold water. Bring to the boil and boil gently for 5 minutes until soft-boiled. Meanwhile, mix together the soured cream and mustard in a bowl.

4. Peel the eggs and cut in half lengthways. Put the latkes on four plates and top each serving with 3 egg halves. Drizzle over the mustard soured cream and spoon the beetroot by the side. Season and serve sprinkled with fennel fronds.

Samphire can be expensive, so it's worth foraging for if you live near a source. There are two types: *marsh samphire*, which grows on shorelines and salt marshes, and *rock samphire* which, unsurprisingly, likes rocky areas. Both have a wonderful crisp texture and saltiness reminiscent of the sea and are best picked young in early summer. Eat raw in salads, steam lightly or briefly sauté in butter.

Poaching eggs can be tricky, but if you follow the instructions below you should get good results. This recipe makes an elegant weekend meal when served with Asian-Style Mash (see page 22) and foraged samphire.

Eggs with Lemongrass Cream

Serves: 4 *Preparation time:* 15 minutes, plus making the stock and 30 minutes infusing *Cooking time:* 25 minutes

8 eggs
1 tsp white wine vinegar
sea salt and freshly ground black pepper

TO SERVE
1 recipe quantity Asian-Style Mash
(see page 22)
2 tbsp snipped chives
1 red chilli, deseeded and chopped
samphire or green beans

LEMONGRASS CREAM SAUCE
2 long lemongrass stalks, bruised
250ml/9fl oz/1 cup Vegetable Stock
(see page 14)
100ml/3½fl oz/scant ½ cup creamy top from
a tin of coconut milk
2 tsp cornflour, mixed with a little water
finely grated zest of 1 large lime and juice
of ½ lime

1. For the sauce, put the lemongrass and stock in a small pan and bring to the boil; boil for 10 minutes until reduced by a third. Remove from the heat and infuse for 30 minutes. Return the pan to the heat, stir in the coconut milk and the cornflour mixture and return to the boil, stirring continuously. Turn the heat down and simmer for 8–10 minutes until reduced and thickened to a creamy consistency. Add the lime zest and juice, season and gently heat through, stirring. Leave to one side.

2. To poach the eggs, fill a large, deep frying pan with just-boiled water from the kettle, at least 5cm/2in deep. When the water starts to simmer, turn the heat down to medium-low, add the vinegar and swirl the water with a spoon. Crack the eggs one at a time into a cup and lower them into the water (you may need to cook them in two batches – if so, reheat very briefly in hot water just before you serve them). Poach the eggs for 2–3 minutes until the whites are set but the yolks remain runny.

3. Remove the lemongrass from the sauce and reheat, if necessary. Divide the Asian-Style Mash onto four plates. Lift the eggs out of the water with a slotted spoon and put on top of the mash, spoon the sauce over and around the edge and sprinkle with chives and chilli. Season with salt and pepper and serve with samphire.

Omelette

An omelette is the ultimate frugal dish: the way it's possible to transform a couple of eggs, a pinch of salt and a tablespoon of butter into a delicious meal is truly satisfying. Fantastic plain, an omelette is also the perfect vehicle for flavourings and fillings – sweet or savoury. A sprinkling of fresh herbs, a filling of grated cheese or sautéed vegetables is all you need. Also try making a thin, one-egg omelette (add 1 teaspoon water), slicing it into narrow strips and serving it on top of oriental soups, rice and noodle dishes. Then there are the flat, open-faced omelettes such as the Italian frittata, Spanish tortilla or the Middle Eastern eggah, which are made with a large proportion of filling ingredients added to the egg, cooked gently on the hob and finished under the grill or in the oven. As with all egg dishes, it's important not to overcook omelettes. It's also essential to cook them in a heavy-based, non-stick pan.

A tortino is an oven-baked version of the Italian frittata, and makes a simple meal or the perfect picnic dish. This tortino has a slightly autumnal flavour with the rich earthiness of dried porcini and leafy greens; you can alter the flavourings to suit the season. A summery alternative might include strips of red pepper, diced courgette and chopped spinach. Whatever you choose, be generous with the ratio of filling to egg.

Rainbow Chard and Parmesan Tortino

Serves: 4   *Preparation time:* 15 minutes, plus 20 minutes soaking and 10 minutes resting   *Cooking time:* 45 minutes

25g/1oz/¼ cup dried porcini
2 tbsp olive oil
1 large onion, finely chopped
3 garlic cloves, finely chopped
270g/9½oz rainbow chard, leaves stripped away from the stalks, thick stalks and stems removed, thin stalks finely sliced

butter, for greasing
2 tsp thyme leaves or 1 tsp dried thyme
60g/2¼oz vegetarian Parmesan cheese, finely grated
7 eggs, lightly beaten
20g/¾oz/⅓ cup day-old breadcrumbs
sea salt and freshly ground black pepper

1. Cover the porcini in just-boiled water and leave to soften for 20 minutes, then drain, reserving the soaking liquor for another recipe. Squeeze out any remaining water and roughly chop the porcini.

2. Meanwhile, heat the oil in a large, non-stick frying pan over a medium heat. Add the onion and fry for 5 minutes until softened. Add the garlic and sliced chard stalks and cook for another 3 minutes, then tip in the porcini and cook for another 5 minutes, followed by the thyme.

3. Preheat the oven to 180°C/350°F/Gas 4. Generously butter a 20cm/8in loose-bottomed cake tin and line the base with baking parchment. Shred the chard leaves and put them in a large mixing bowl with the onion mixture. Add the Parmesan, reserving 2 tablespoons, and the eggs. Season well with salt and pepper and stir until combined.

4. Sprinkle half the breadcrumbs in an even layer into the base of the tin. Pour the egg mixture into the tin, so everything is evenly distributed, and sprinkle with the remaining breadcrumbs and the reserved Parmesan. Bake for 35–40 minutes until set. Leave the tortino to rest in the tin for 10 minutes before removing it. Serve cut into wedges.

Pictured on page 127.

▶▶ Eggah

Eggah is a Middle Eastern version of a Spanish tortilla or Italian frittata. Sauté **1 large diced courgette** in **2 tsp olive oil** in a large, non-stick, heavy-based, ovenproof frying pan for 5 minutes until softened and slightly coloured. Tip into a large bowl with **140g/5oz chopped baby spinach leaves**, **1 bunch of chopped spring onions**, **2 handfuls of chopped coriander leaves**, **1 tsp allspice** and **½ tsp cumin seeds**. Beat **8 large eggs** and season well with **salt** and **pepper**. Pour the egg mixture over the spinach mixture and stir until combined. Heat **2 tsp olive oil** in the frying pan over a medium-low heat. Pour in the egg mixture and cook for 10 minutes until the base is light golden and set. Preheat the grill to medium and put the frying pan under the grill for 3 minutes, or until set. Serve cut into wedges.

▶▶ Sous-Vide Omelette

This is my home-style version of sous-vide (the method of cooking food in a vacuum-sealed bag in a water bath), which doesn't require any special equipment. It's an interesting concept and produces an omelette with a soft, creamy consistency. For two people, pour just-boiled water into a large, deep sauté pan until nearly full and set over a low heat – the water should be just simmering. Whisk together **4 eggs** with **1 tbsp single cream** and add **1 tbsp chopped chives** and season with **salt** and **pepper**. Pour the mixture into a zip-lock freezer bag, squeeze out as much air as possible and seal. Fold the top of the bag over a couple of times to make a small rectangular parcel. Put the parcel in the water and press down with a spatula until submerged, cover and simmer the eggs for 8–10 minutes until the omelette is just set. Carefully remove the bag from the water and let the omelette settle in the bottom of the bag. Gently slide the omelette onto serving plates.

▶▶ Sushi Rolls

Use a thin, **one-egg omelette** to encase rice and/or vegetable rolls instead of nori sheets. Trim the omelette to make a square and arrange stir-fried **springs onions**, **red pepper** and **asparagus** down the middle. Roll up the omelette and cut into 2.5cm/1in lengths, stand the rolls up on their end and serve with **soy sauce** and **pickled ginger**.

Chapter 6
Slice of Cheese (and Other Dairy)

For the home cook, dairy products are incredibly varied and add a wonderful flavour and texture to all manner of dishes. Cheeses made from cows', ewes', goats' or even buffalos' milk will all have individual characteristics depending on where they're from, how they're produced and the way they're matured. The recipes in this chapter encapsulate this versatility, such as the creamy yet potent Potted Cheese with Elderflower Pears, fresh and light Ricotta and Wild Greens Dumplings and nutty-tasting Beet Top, Spring Onion and Gruyère Tart.

This smooth pâté makes use of any leftover or tail-end bits of cheese you might have in the fridge. You can use a single type of goats', cows' or sheep's cheese, or try a combination: a piquant blue; a crumbly, mature hard cheese; or a soft, creamy one are all possibilities, but look for a balance of flavours. I wanted to make use of the short elderflower season by poaching the pears in an elderflower-infused syrup. The result is delicately perfumed, succulent fruit that complements the creamy tanginess of the potted cheese.

Potted Cheese with Elderflower Pears

Serves: 4   *Preparation time:* 15 minutes, plus making the syrup and chilling
Cooking time: 20 minutes

250ml/9fl oz/1 cup Elderflower Syrup
   (see page 25)
4 just-ripe but not mushy pears, peeled and
   cut in half lengthways
light rye bread, toasted, to serve

POTTED CHEESE
85g/3oz very soft butter
125g/4½oz Dolcelatte, cut into small pieces
40g/1½oz vegetarian Parmesan cheese, grated
2 tbsp semi-dry flowery white wine or sherry
freshly ground black pepper

1. Put the elderflower syrup in a saucepan with 300ml/10½fl oz/scant 1¼ cups water. Add the pears – they should be just covered by the liquid, and if necessary add a little more water, but you don't want the syrup to be too diluted. Bring to a gentle boil, then turn the heat down and simmer, part-covered, for 15–20 minutes, until the pears are tender. Remove from the heat and leave the pears to cool in the syrup.

2. Meanwhile, put the butter, cheese and wine in a mixing bowl, and beat with a wooden spoon until combined. Season with pepper, and spoon the mixture into four small ramekins. Smooth the top and chill until firm. Remove the potted cheese from the fridge 20 minutes before serving to soften, and serve with the poached pears and toast.

Elderflowers

grow profusely but have a relatively short season, so make the most of the delicately perfumed clusters of creamy-white flowers in early to mid-summer (see page 25). Early autumn welcomes the elderberry with its distinctive heads of small, deep purple berries. The berries have to be cooked and make a delicious syrup, pie filling mixed with other seasonal fruit, or jam.

There's a knack to opening a fresh coconut, and it requires a steady hand. Carefully bore two holes through the 'eyes' in the top with a screwdriver or drill, and drain the liquid (it makes a super-hydrating drink). Using a wooden mallet or the blunt side of a heavy blade, firmly strike the coconut around its equator until it splits in half, then cut the coconut meat from the outer shell and brown skin.

Tandoori Halloumi with Coconut and Pineapple Salad

Serves: 4 *Preparation time:* 15 minutes *Cooking time:* 5 minutes

3 tbsp tandoori spice mix
325g/11½oz halloumi, rinsed, patted dry and
    sliced lengthways into 8 thick slices
½ pineapple, skin removed, cored and cut into
    bite-sized pieces
250g/9oz/2 cups drained tinned chickpeas or
    cooked dried chickpeas (see pages 8–9)

1–2 long green chillies, deseeded and diced
1 small red onion, diced
55g/2oz fresh coconut, coarsely grated
2 handfuls of coriander leaves, chopped
juice of 1½–2 limes
1 tbsp sunflower oil
sea salt and freshly ground black pepper

1. Sprinkle the spice mix over a plate and season with pepper. Coat both sides of each halloumi slice in the spices and leave to one side.

2. Put the pineapple, chickpeas, green chillies, red onion, fresh coconut and coriander in a serving bowl. Squeeze over the smaller quantity of lime juice, and season with salt and pepper. Toss until everything is combined, then taste, adding more lime juice and/or seasoning if needed.

3. Heat the oil in a large, non-stick frying pan over a medium heat. Cook the halloumi for 3–4 minutes, turning once, until softened and slightly coloured. Serve immediately with the salad.

An alternative way to open a coconut is to freeze it overnight. The next day, crack the shell as above and the flesh should come away more easily from the shell and brown skin.

This is a great summer salad with a lively combination of flavours: cooling, sweet watermelon; tangy lime juice; and slight heat from the fresh chilli – all counterbalanced by the salty sharpness of the feta cheese. Homemade Paneer (see page 17) works well instead of the feta, too.

Watermelon, Feta and Mint Salad

Serves: 4   Preparation time: 15 minutes

550g/1lb 4oz watermelon, seeds removed if you like, cut into 2cm/¾in cubes
1 small red onion, thinly sliced into rings
20 pitted black olives
125g/4½oz sheep's feta cheese or Homemade Paneer (see page 17), cubed
1 small handful of mint leaves

1 long red chilli, deseeded and thinly sliced into rounds
juice and pared rind of 1 small lime, cut into very fine strips
2–3 tbsp extra virgin olive oil
sea salt and freshly ground black pepper
warm flatbreads, to serve

1. Put the watermelon on a large serving plate and scatter the red onion, olives, feta, mint and chilli over the top.

2. Drizzle the lime juice over the salad and sprinkle with the strips of lime rind. Drizzle with the olive oil, to taste, and season with salt and pepper. Serve at room temperature with warm flatbreads.

Extend the life of fresh chillies by storing them in an airtight container in the freezer. Defrost briefly to make them easier to slice before using in a recipe.

Mint is a versatile addition to a kitchen garden, but it's also a vigorous herb that needs containing, otherwise it can become too prolific. Grow it in pots, or alternatively plant the pot it comes in — making sure it allows enough room for growth — straight into the earth. There are many varieties of mint and it's worth checking out some of the more unusual ones, such as chocolate or apple!

Try to use a crumbly goats' cheese rather than a soft, runny one to make these thick, savoury pancakes. They are good eaten simply – for example, spread with garlic butter or with a herb-infused yogurt – but also make a more substantial meal when served with Pomegranate Salsa (see page 21).

Goats' Cheese Pancakes

Serves: 4   *Preparation time:* 20 minutes   *Cooking time:* 1 hour

150g/5½oz/scant 1¼ cups self-raising flour
1 tsp baking powder
½ tsp sea salt
3 eggs, separated
150ml/5fl oz/scant ⅔ cup milk
50g/1¾oz butter, melted
100g/3½oz rindless goats' cheese, crumbled

3 handfuls of baby spinach or young sea beet
    leaves, finely chopped
5 spring onions, finely sliced
3 tbsp chopped coriander leaves
sunflower oil, for frying
freshly ground black pepper
Pomegranate Salsa (see page 21), to serve

1. Mix together the flour, baking powder and salt in a large mixing bowl. Using a balloon whisk, mix in the egg yolks, milk and melted butter, then stir in the goats' cheese, spinach, spring onions and coriander. Season with pepper.

2. Whisk the eggs whites to soft peaks and gently fold them into the goats' cheese batter.

3. Pour a little oil into a large, non-stick, heavy-based frying pan and put over a medium heat. For each pancake, ladle in 3 tablespoons of batter and cook for 4–5 minutes, turning once, until golden. Drain on kitchen paper and keep warm in a low oven. Repeat, adding more oil to the pan as needed until the batter is used up; it should make about 12 pancakes. Serve with the Pomegranate Salsa.

If a recipe calls for just the green part of spring onions, don't ditch the white parts – regrow them. Stand them in a glass with about 5cm/2in water. Put in a light place and watch the green parts sprout, topping up the glass with more water when necessary. After about 5 days the green parts will be ready to cut and use again – you can do this a couple of times before the spring onion runs out of momentum.

To me, curries often taste better the day after making, and this spicy lentil–tomato sauce is no exception. A day allows the spices time to get to know each other; to mingle and meld. Serve with a scattering of crumbled Homemade Paneer (see page 17), Mango Chutney (see page 19) and warmed naan bread. A handful of Crispy Onions and Ginger (see page 23) would be good, too.

Lentil Sambar with Paneer

Serves: 4 *Preparation time:* 15 minutes *Cooking time:* 55 minutes

90g/3¼oz/⅓ cup dried split red lentils, rinsed
7 garlic cloves, peeled
30g/1oz root ginger, peeled and chopped
1 red chilli
6 tbsp rapeseed or vegetable oil
2 onions, chopped
2 tbsp Curry Spice Mix (see page 15)
5 vine-ripened tomatoes, roughly chopped
2 tsp soft brown sugar
½ tsp dried chilli flakes (optional)

2 tbsp tamarind paste or lemon juice
sea salt and freshly ground black pepper

TO SERVE
½ recipe quantity Homemade Paneer
  (see page 17), crumbled
3 tbsp chopped coriander leaves
Crispy Onions and Ginger (see page 23),
  optional
Mango Chutney (see page 19), optional

1. Put the lentils in a pan and cover generously with water. Bring to the boil, then turn the heat down and simmer, part-covered, for 15 minutes until tender. Drain and leave to one side.

2. Blend the garlic, ginger and red chilli with 4 tablespoons water until smooth. Leave to one side.

3. Heat the oil in a saucepan over a medium heat. Add the onions and cook for 15 minutes, stirring occasionally, until just beginning to colour. Add the spice mix and the garlic paste and cook for another 5 minutes, stirring regularly.

4. Stir in the tomatoes, sugar, chilli flakes, if using, tamarind, cooked lentils and 125ml/4fl oz/½ cup water, and bring to the boil. Turn the heat down slightly and simmer for 15 minutes, part-covered, until reduced to a thick sauce. Season with salt and pepper and sprinkle with the paneer, coriander and Crispy Onions and Ginger, if using. Serve with spoonfuls of mango chutney.

To freeze the sambar, omit the paneer and coriander and freeze flat in zip-lock bags. There's no need to defrost; add a splash of water and heat gently in a covered pan.

Wild greens are a good alternative to cultivated spinach. Opt for young leaves, which are less bitter; you can reduce bitterness by soaking them in salted water for 30 minutes, then drain and rinse before cooking.

Ricotta and Wild Greens Dumplings

Serves: 4   **Preparation time:** 20 minutes   **Cooking time:** 30 minutes

1 tbsp olive oil
125g/4½oz wild greens, such as Good King Henry, wild watercress, Alexanders or sea beet (or double the quantity of spinach), stems removed, leaves shredded
125g/4½oz baby spinach leaves, shredded
1 large egg, separated
250g/9oz ricotta cheese, drained
40g/1½oz vegetarian Parmesan cheese, grated
60g/2¼oz/½ cup plain flour, plus extra for dusting

2 tbsp chopped basil leaves, plus extra to serve
sea salt and freshly ground black pepper

TOMATO SAUCE
2 tbsp olive oil
2 large garlic cloves, finely chopped
800g/1lb 12oz/3 cups tinned chopped tomatoes
3 large basil sprigs
1 tbsp tomato purée
1 tsp sugar

1. To make the tomato sauce, put the oil and garlic in a large saucepan over a medium-low heat and cook gently for 1 minute until the garlic is softened but not coloured. Add the tomatoes and basil sprigs and bring to a gentle boil, then turn the heat down, stir in the tomato purée and sugar, and simmer, part-covered, for 10 minutes until reduced and thickened. Season with salt and pepper.

2. Meanwhile, make the dumplings. Heat the oil in a large, non-stick frying pan over a medium heat. Add the wild greens and spinach and sauté for 3 minutes, stirring regularly, until wilted and tender. Mix the greens with the egg yolk, ricotta, Parmesan, flour and basil, then season with salt and pepper. Whisk the egg white with an electric whisk until it forms stiff peaks, then fold it gently into the ricotta mixture.

3. Bring a large pan of salted water to the boil. Using floured hands, make small balls about the size of a large walnut with the ricotta mixture; it should make about 20 balls. Add the balls to the gently boiling water in four batches and cook for 4–5 minutes, turning them occasionally, until just firm. Drain on kitchen paper and keep warm in a low oven while you cook the remaining dumplings.

4. Reheat the tomato sauce, if needed, and remove the basil sprigs. Serve the ricotta and wild greens dumplings on top of the tomato sauce with a sprinkling of extra basil.

Look out for *Good King Henry*, with its triangular leaves and spiky flowers, in rich soil or cultivated land. It's a generous plant, providing edible leaves pretty much all year round – though the smaller, younger leaves are preferable. The young stems are also edible, hence the plant's nickname of poor man's asparagus. In the home garden it is low maintenance and largely pest resistant.

To grow garlic, split a bulb into cloves. Plant the cloves, pointed end up, 1cm/½in deep and 12cm/4½in apart in pots or free-draining soil in late autumn. Feed and water when dry throughout the growing season. Remove any flower heads; like onion or chive flowers these are edible, too. It is ready for harvesting when the leaves start to wilt and turn yellow. Eat fresh or leave to dry in a cool, dry place.

If you have a loaf that is just past its best, avoid throwing it away by using it in this savoury, cheesy bread pudding. Ideally, the loaf should have a slightly open-textured crumb so it absorbs the cheese and egg mixture and doesn't become too dense when baked. Don't ditch the crusts; they can be turned into breadcrumbs and frozen until you need them. Feel free to replace the Cheddar with whatever cheese you have in the fridge, or try a mixture of different ones.

Cheese and Pepper Strata

Serves: 4 *Preparation time:* 15 minutes, plus 10 minutes standing
Cooking time: 1 hour

1 red pepper, deseeded and sliced
1 yellow pepper, deseeded and sliced
2 tbsp olive oil
375g/13oz slightly stale, open-textured bread,
   crusts removed, sliced and cut into squares
2 garlic cloves, crushed
6 spring onions, sliced

1 large handful of basil leaves
175g/6oz mature Cheddar or cheese of choice,
   coarsely grated
6 eggs, lightly beaten
300ml/10½fl oz/scant 1¼ cups milk
sea salt and freshly ground black pepper

1. Preheat the oven to 180°C/350°F/Gas 4. Brush the peppers with the oil. Heat a large griddle pan over a high heat and griddle the peppers for 6–8 minutes, turning occasionally, until tender and starting to blacken in places. You may need to cook the peppers in batches.

2. Meanwhile, put half the bread in a large, shallow ovenproof dish. Top the bread with an even layer of cooked pepper, garlic, spring onions, basil and half the Cheddar.

3. Whisk together the eggs and milk and season with salt and pepper. Pour half the mixture into the dish, making sure the bread is evenly covered. Top with the remaining bread and pour the rest of the egg and milk mixture over, pressing the bread down so it is thoroughly soaked. Scatter the remaining cheese over and leave to stand for 10 minutes. Bake for 35–40 minutes until the cheese has melted and is golden on top.

To extend the life of shop-bought pots of fresh herbs during the warmer months, plant in larger pots or in the garden, then water regularly and wait for the new growth.

If you find beetroot with the stems and leaves still intact, they make a good alternative to chard, cavolo nero or spinach. Use them promptly and discard any that are damaged or wrinkly. I've splashed out on Gruyère cheese, but you could use mature Cheddar or crumbly goats' or sheep's cheese instead.

Beet Top, Spring Onion and Gruyère Tart

Serves: 4–6   **Preparation time:** 20 minutes, plus making the pastry
Cooking time: 1 hour 10 minutes

butter, for greasing
1 recipe quantity Shortcrust Pastry
   (see page 13)
plain flour, for dusting

FILLING
1 tbsp sunflower oil
2 bunches of spring onions, sliced,
   green and white parts kept separate

tops from 4 large raw beetroot, stems and
   leaves thinly sliced and separated
1 handful of wild garlic leaves (see page 55)
   or chives, roughly chopped
3 large eggs, lightly beaten
250ml/9fl oz/1 cup full-fat milk
115g/4oz Gruyère cheese, coarsely grated
sea salt and freshly ground black pepper

1. Preheat the oven to 190°C/375°F/Gas 5 and heat a baking sheet. Grease a 28cm/11¼in flan tin.

2. Roll the pastry out on a lightly floured work surface until about 5mm/¼in thick. Use the pastry to line the prepared tin, leaving a slight overhang. Line the pastry with foil and weigh down with baking beans. Put the tin on the preheated baking sheet and bake for 15 minutes. Remove the foil and beans and return the tin to the oven for another 15 minutes until the pastry is cooked and light golden.

3. Meanwhile, make the filling. Heat the oil in a large frying pan over a medium heat. Add the white part of the spring onions and beet stems and cook for 2 minutes until tender. Add the green part of the spring onions, beet leaves and wild garlic (if using chives, stir them into the egg and milk mixture, see below) and cook for another 2 minutes until just softened.

4. Whisk together the eggs and milk in a jug and season with salt and pepper. Spoon the spring onion mixture into the pastry case and scatter the cheese over in an even layer. Pour in the egg mixture, then return to the oven for 40 minutes until the filling is just set. Serve cut into wedges.

Use dried beans if you don't have baking beans – soya beans are good. They can be reused, too – leave them to cool and store in an airtight container until the next time.

Beetroot makes an attractive addition to a vegetable bed. Sow the seeds in drills about 2cm/¾in deep and cover with compost. Water the soil and thin out the seedlings when they're about 2.5cm/1in tall, leaving a 12cm/4½in gap between them. The beetroot will be ready to harvest in about 3 months. Don't throw the leaves away, as they are delicious cooked and eaten like chard or spinach.

This always goes down a storm at home. It's like macaroni cheese but with a lighter, stock-based cheese sauce, rather than a milky one. Conchiglie are shell-shaped pasta and are perfect for capturing cheesy or creamy sauces, but you could use any type of short-cut, dried pasta you have in the cupboard.

Conchiglie and Broccoli Gratin

Serves: *4* **Preparation time:** *20 minutes, plus making the stock*
Cooking time: *30 minutes*

325g/11½oz dried conchiglie
1 large head of broccoli, thick stem removed,
    cut into small florets
600ml/21fl oz/scant 2½ cups Vegetable Stock
    (see page 14)
100ml/3½fl oz/scant ½ cup whipping cream
30g/1oz butter
2 large garlic cloves, finely chopped

2 tbsp plain flour
2 tsp Dijon mustard
150g/5½oz mixture of hard cheeses,
    such as Gruyère and mature Cheddar,
    coarsely grated
4 tbsp day-old breadcrumbs
sea salt and freshly ground black pepper

1. Preheat the oven to 180°C/350°F/Gas 4. Cook the pasta in plenty of boiling salted water, following the pack instructions, until al dente. Three minutes before the pasta is ready, add the broccoli florets to the pan. Drain the pasta and broccoli and tip them into a large, shallow ovenproof dish.

2. Meanwhile, bring the stock to the boil in a separate pan and boil gently until reduced to 500ml/17fl oz/2 cups; this will help to concentrate its flavour. Remove from the heat and stir in the cream.

3. Melt the butter in a heavy-based pan over a medium-low heat. Add the garlic and cook for 1 minute until softened. Stir in the flour with a wooden spoon and cook for 1 minute, then gradually mix in the stock mixture, stirring continuously to make a sauce the consistency of thin custard. Add the mustard and three-quarters of the cheese and season with salt and pepper.

4. Pour the sauce over the pasta and broccoli in the dish and turn until everything is combined. Sprinkle over the remaining cheese and the breadcrumbs and bake for 15–20 minutes until golden and crisp on top.

Keep the thick broccoli stalk for use in another recipe. Peel and cut into slices to add to stir-fries, soups and stews.

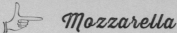 **Mozzarella**

A trip to an Italian delicatessen will reveal porcelain-white balls of mozzarella in a stunning range of shapes and sizes floating in tubs of whey or water. Mozzarella ranges from the single-bite globes known as bocconcini to the larger, cream-filled balls of burrata, and much more in between. Star of the show is mozzarella di bufala Campana (DOP), made with buffalo milk using a protected, age-old method. In fact, all mozzarella was once made with buffalo milk, but cows' milk is now most common. This southern Italian fresh, unripened cheese with a milky, slightly sour edge and elastic texture is equally happy used as a main ingredient in classic salads – such as insalata Caprese, when it is combined with tomato and basil – as it is in a cooked dish, such as melanzane alla Parmigiana (baked layers of aubergine, tomato, mozzarella and Parmesan); its unique melting properties also make it a must-have topping on a pizza.

Full of summer flavours, this roasted vegetable, mozzarella and croûton panzanella is a twist on the classic uncooked Italian salad. It's perfect for using up a glut of summer veg and calls for young, fresh cloves of garlic.

Roasted Panzanella

Serves: *4–6*   **Preparation time:** *20 minutes*   **Cooking time:** *40 minutes*

4 tbsp olive oil
2 red peppers, halved and deseeded, each
   half cut into 3 wedges
2 yellow peppers, halved and deseeded,
   each half cut into 3 wedges
2 red onions, halved and cut into wedges
2 courgettes, cut into 1cm/½in diagonal slices
6 vine-ripened tomatoes, deseeded and
   quartered
6 garlic cloves, 2 peeled and 4 unpeeled
1 loaf day-old ciabatta or other crusty bread,
   halved lengthways, then halved again
   crossways

½ tsp cumin seeds
1 handful each of basil and oregano leaves
200g/7oz mozzarella cheese, drained and torn
   into bite-sized pieces
sea salt and freshly ground black pepper

DRESSING
4 tbsp extra virgin olive oil
3 tbsp balsamic vinegar

1. Preheat the oven to 200°C/400°F/Gas 6. Put the olive oil in a large bowl and add the peppers, onions, courgettes and tomatoes, season with salt and pepper, and turn to coat everything in the oil. Tip the vegetables into two large roasting tins and spread out in an even layer. Add the 4 unpeeled garlic cloves and roast for 20 minutes, or until the garlic is very soft. Remove the garlic and tomatoes from the roasting tins and leave to one side. Turn the rest of the vegetables in the tins and return them to the oven for a further 20 minutes until tender and slightly browned around the edges.

2. Meanwhile, heat a large griddle pan over a medium heat. Griddle the ciabatta for 6 minutes, turning once, until toasted and blackened in places. Cut the remaining peeled garlic in half, rub the cut half over the toasted ciabatta and leave to cool.

3. To make the dressing, put the ingredients in a jar and season with salt and pepper. Squeeze the roasted garlic out of its papery shell and finely chop. Add the garlic to the dressing, cover and shake well until combined. Put the roasted vegetables on a large serving plate. Tear the ciabatta into bite-sized pieces and scatter them over the top with the cumin seeds, herbs and mozzarella. Spoon the dressing over and serve.

Pictured on page 149.

Scamorza, Orzo and Basil Oil Salad

I'm generally not a fan of pasta salads, but this is something else. Scamorza, a form of smoked mozzarella with a firmer texture, is delicious cubed and stirred into cooked **250g/9oz/scant 2 cups orzo** pasta. About **150g/5½oz scamorza** will do. Add **2 small sliced avocados**, **3 deseeded and diced tomatoes** and **2 handfuls of rocket leaves**. For the dressing, blend **5 tbsp extra virgin olive oil** with **3 handfuls of basil leaves**, **1 garlic clove**, **the juice of 1 large lemon** and **salt** and **pepper** until combined. Spoon it over the salad and toss until combined. Scatter over **2 tbsp toasted pine nuts** (see page 18) to serve.

Chinese Black Bean and Mozzarella Salad

A clash of cultures maybe, but this works so well. Soak **3 tbsp Chinese fermented black beans** in just-boiled water for 20 minutes, then drain (save the stock for another recipe). Meanwhile, mix together **2 tbsp sunflower oil**, **1 tsp sesame oil** and **2 tsp light soy sauce** in a bowl. Stir in **1 finely chopped spring onion**, **½ chopped and deseeded red chilli**, **1 tsp peeled and finely chopped root ginger** and the drained black beans. Put **300g/10½oz drained and thickly sliced mozzarella cheese** in a bowl and spoon the dressing over the top. Scatter over **1 handful each of chopped coriander and basil leaves**.

Mozzarella with Szechuan Pepper

A warm salad with a mouth-tingling dressing: toast **1 tsp Szechuan peppercorns** in a large, dry frying pan for 1 minute until aromatic. Remove from the pan and grind with **½ tsp sea salt**. Add **2 tbsp olive oil** to the pan and fry **2 diagonally sliced yellow courgettes** for 5 minutes, or until tender and starting to colour. Transfer to a serving plate with any juices in the pan and scatter over **150g/5½oz mozzarella cheese**, torn into pieces. Sprinkle with as much of the Szechuan salt as you like.

Chapter 7
Box of Veg

Vegetables offer an almost infinite number of culinary possibilities to the home cook and are much, much more than just a side dish. The recipes in this chapter will open your eyes to new possibilities, from the stunning Potato and Borage Salad, to golden, crisp Pea and Tofu Fritters and aromatic Moroccan Slow-Cooked Vegetables. When it comes to buying vegetables, seasonal is best; not only will they be kinder on the purse, they'll taste better too. That said, don't forget the ultimate convenience food – frozen veg.

Cornflower-blue, star-shaped borage flowers look attractive and have a fresh taste reminiscent of cucumber – and what's more, the leaves of this annual herb are edible too. I also like to add a handful of finely chopped wild or cultivated sorrel leaves to the salad dressing in place of the lemon zest. It has a citrusy sharpness that works well with creamy sauces and resembles young, pointed spinach leaves. Find it on grassland and along banks from spring to late autumn.

Potato and Borage Salad

Serves: 4   *Preparation time:* 15 minutes   *Cooking time:* 16 minutes

650g/1lb 7oz new potatoes, scrubbed and
   halved if large
4 eggs
1 handful of borage flowers and young leaves,
   leaves shredded
1 small red onion, cut into rings
10 radishes, thinly sliced
2 tbsp extra virgin olive oil
1 small handful of wild fennel fronds or dill,
   snipped
sea salt and freshly ground black pepper

LEMON CREAM
100ml/3½fl oz/scant ½ cup low-fat
   natural yogurt
2 tbsp mayonnaise
juice and finely grated zest of 1 small lemon
2 tsp wholegrain mustard

Serve with the Easter Egg Pies (see page 120).

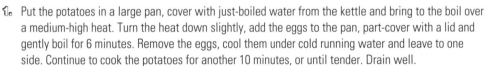

1. Put the potatoes in a large pan, cover with just-boiled water from the kettle and bring to the boil over a medium-high heat. Turn the heat down slightly, add the eggs to the pan, part-cover with a lid and gently boil for 6 minutes. Remove the eggs, cool them under cold running water and leave to one side. Continue to cook the potatoes for another 10 minutes, or until tender. Drain well.

2. Meanwhile, mix together the ingredients for the lemon cream with 2 tablespoons water, season with salt and pepper and leave to one side.

3. Cut the potatoes into bite-sized pieces and place in a serving bowl with the borage leaves. Scatter over the red onion and radishes, drizzle the oil over the top and turn lightly until combined. Drizzle over half of the lemon cream.

4. Peel and roughly mash the eggs, then pile them on top of the potatoes. Scatter the fennel fronds and borage flowers over. Serve the salad with the remaining lemon cream by the side.

Borage

is an annual herb that
blooms from spring onwards,
prolonged with regular dead-heading.
It is self-seeding, often found growing
wild, and also makes an attractive garden
plant. Pollinating bees love it, so it is a good
companion to tomatoes and strawberries.
Both the flowers and young leaves are
edible but the latter (as well as the
stems) can become prickly later
on in the season.

This main-meal salad takes all the elements of the classic Lebanese fattoush but gives it a Mexican twist – so there are toasted corn tortillas, chunks of avocado, tangy lime juice and lots of fresh coriander. It's best dressed just before serving so the toasted tortillas remain crisp, and at room temperature to let the flavours sing through.

Mexican Fattoush

Serves: 4 *Preparation time:* 15 minutes *Cooking time:* 16 minutes

2 soft corn tortillas
5 large vine-ripened tomatoes, deseeded and cut into chunks
1 large yellow pepper, deseeded and cut into chunks
1 small red onion, thinly sliced into rings
2 avocados, pitted, peeled and cut into chunks
1 handful of coriander leaves, chopped

1 handful of mint leaves, chopped
1 red chilli, deseeded and diced (optional)

DRESSING
3 tbsp extra virgin olive oil, plus extra for brushing
juice of 1 lime
sea salt and freshly ground black pepper

1. Lightly brush both sides of each tortilla with olive oil. Heat a large, non-stick frying pan over a medium-low heat and toast the tortillas one at a time for 3–4 minutes, turning once, until crisp on both sides. Leave to cool and crisp up further, then tear them up roughly.

2. Put the tomatoes, yellow pepper, onion and avocados in a shallow serving bowl, then scatter the herbs over the top.

3. Mix together the ingredients for the dressing and season with salt and pepper. Pour the dressing over the salad and toss gently until combined. Scatter the toasted tortillas and chilli (if using) over, toss again and serve immediately.

To keep a year-round supply of fresh herbs, remove the leaves from their stalks and freeze them – chopped or whole – spread out in a single layer on a baking sheet. The stalks can be frozen separately and ground or finely chopped for use in soups and stews. You can also freeze fresh herbs in ice cube trays suspended in a little water.

Great served with the Semolina and Nut Milk Gnocchi (see page 96), this dish is highly adaptable, making a delicious topping on bruschetta, served with pasta or rice for a more substantial meal, or as part of a selection of mezes. It will keep in the fridge for up to 3 days, but is best served at room temperature or warm.

Aubergine Meze

Serves: 4   **Preparation time:** 10 minutes   **Cooking time:** 20 minutes

6 tbsp olive oil
1 large aubergine, diced
4 garlic cloves, finely chopped
4cm/1½in piece of root ginger, peeled
  and finely grated
1 tsp cumin seeds

2 tsp ground coriander
1 tsp turmeric
3 tomatoes, deseeded and chopped
juice of 1 lemon
sea salt and freshly ground black pepper

1. Heat the olive oil in a large, non-stick frying pan over a medium heat. Add the aubergine and fry for 10 minutes, turning occasionally, until golden all over and tender. Stir in the garlic, ginger and cumin seeds and cook for another minute until the garlic has softened.

2. Add the ground spices, tomatoes and 5 tablespoons water and bring to a gentle boil, then turn the heat down and simmer for 10 minutes, stirring occasionally, until reduced and thickened. Remove from the heat, stir in the lemon juice and season with salt and pepper. Serve warm or at room temperature.

It's no longer necessary to salt aubergines before you use them to extract the bitter juices, because over the years any bitterness has been bred out of them. However, salting does curb the amount of oil the aubergine absorbs when fried.

This dish of braised summer vegetables has a Moroccan feel with the tangy preserved lemons, olives and spices. I like to serve the vegetables with crisp slices of griddled polenta (see page 86), but steamed couscous is good, too.

Moroccan Slow-Cooked Vegetables

Serves: 4–6   *Preparation time:* 15 minutes, plus making the preserved lemons and 15 minutes soaking   *Cooking time:* 55 minutes

40g/1½oz sundried tomatoes, thickly sliced
2 tsp Poor Man's Saffron (see page 76) or a
   large pinch of saffron
3 tbsp olive oil
1 large onion, sliced
2 large fennel bulbs, fronds trimmed and
   reserved, halved lengthways and cut into
   1cm/½in wedges
3 courgettes, cut into large bite-sized chunks
100g/3½oz/¾ cup small black pitted olives

1 tsp turmeric
1 tsp vegetable bouillon powder
2 tbsp thyme leaves
1 tsp dried thyme
1 recipe quantity Quick Preserved Lemons
   (see page 24)
sea salt and freshly ground black pepper
1 recipe quantity Polenta Bruschetta
   (see page 86), to serve

1. Soak the sundried tomatoes and Poor Man's Saffron in 400ml/14fl oz/1⅔ cups hot water for 15 minutes.

2. Meanwhile, heat the olive oil in a large, heavy-based saucepan over a medium-low heat. Add the onion and cook, covered, for 10 minutes, stirring occasionally, until softened. Add the fennel and cook for another 5 minutes until starting to soften.

3. Add the courgettes, olives and sundried tomatoes with their saffron soaking water and bring to the boil. Stir in the turmeric, bouillon powder and thyme, turn the heat down to low and simmer, part-covered, for 30 minutes, stirring occasionally. Add the preserved lemons and cook, uncovered, for another 10 minutes until the sauce has reduced and thickened and the vegetables are tender. Season with salt and pepper, and serve with the Polenta Bruschetta, sprinkled with reserved fennel fronds.

Olives are also used in the Paella with Poor Man's Saffron (see page 76).

It's worth harvesting wild fennel flowers for use in the kitchen or for planting next year. Put a small paper bag over the flower head, secure with a rubber band, turn upside down and leave for a few weeks in a cool, dry place. When dry, shake the flower heads to remove the seeds.

This makes a light, summery meal or starter. After cooking the broad beans, it's best to remove their grey outer shell, which can be tough, to reveal the tender green bean inside. The beans are then stirred into a lemony goats' cheese mousse with some diced kohlrabi. I'd shied away from the alien-looking kohlrabi until fairly recently, but I'm pleasantly surprised at how good it tastes – like a cross between a radish and a turnip – with a fresh, crisp texture.

Broad Bean and Goats' Cheese Crostini

Serves: 4   *Preparation time:* 15 minutes, plus making the Quick Preserved Lemons (optional)   *Cooking time:* 10 minutes

500g/1lb 2oz/4 cups shelled broad beans
75g/2½oz/½ cup peeled and diced kohlrabi
1 handful of mint leaves, chopped
8 thick slices of country-style bread/ciabatta
1 large garlic clove, halved
½ small red onion, thinly sliced into rounds

GOATS' CHEESE MOUSSE
225g/8oz fresh, mild goats' cheese
2 tsp finely chopped Quick Preserved Lemons (see page 24), or zest of 1 lemon
2 tbsp milk
2 tbsp olive oil
sea salt and freshly ground black pepper

1. Bring a pan of salted water to the boil over a high heat. Add the broad beans and boil gently for 2–3 minutes until tender, then drain and refresh under cold running water. When cool, peel off the grey outer skins and put the beans in a bowl with the kohlrabi and half of the mint.

2. While the beans are cooking, make the goats' cheese mousse. Beat together the goats' cheese, preserved lemons, milk and olive oil, then season with salt and pepper. Fold into the broad bean mixture.

3. Toast the bread and rub one side of each slice with the cut side of the garlic. Serve the toast topped with the broad bean mixture and scatter the onion and remaining mint over.

Use leftover herbs to make herbal tea infusions: mint, fennel, nettle, lemon balm and lemon verbena are particularly good.

Kohlrabi

is a brassica with a swollen, bulb-like root that grows above ground and has thick, leafy stalks. It is a fast grower, taking about 10 weeks from seed until harvest. Both the bulb and the leaves are edible: serve the former grated into salads or lightly sautéed in butter; the leaves can be served like cabbage. Look for the purple variety, which will add glorious colour to the garden.

These oriental-inspired fritters come with my take on the Japanese ponzu dipping sauce, which is a sweet-sour-salty combination of citrus juice, soy sauce and brown sugar.

Pea and Tofu Fritters

Serves: *4*   **Preparation time:** *20 minutes*   **Cooking time:** *25 minutes*

185g/6½oz firm tofu, drained, patted dry and
  coarsely grated
200g/7oz/heaped 1¼ cups fresh shelled or
  frozen peas, defrosted if frozen
6 spring onions, finely chopped
2 large garlic cloves, crushed
2.5cm/1in piece of root ginger, grated
  (no need to peel)
½ tsp dried chilli flakes
110g/3¾oz/scant 1 cup plain flour

3 eggs, lightly beaten
200ml/7fl oz/scant 1 cup sunflower oil
sea salt and freshly ground black pepper
4 handfuls of pea shoots, to serve

PONZU DIPPING SAUCE
6 tbsp light soy sauce or tamari
6 tbsp fresh orange juice
2 tbsp lemon juice or rice vinegar
4 tsp soft light brown sugar

1. Squeeze the grated tofu in a clean tea towel to remove any excess water and tip into a bowl with the peas, 5 of the spring onions, garlic, ginger and chilli flakes and mix together.

2. Put the flour in a separate bowl, make a well in the centre and add the beaten eggs. Gradually mix the eggs into the flour until you have a thick, smooth batter, then stir in the pea mixture and season well with salt and pepper.

3. Heat the oil in a large, deep frying pan over a medium heat. Spoon heaped tablespoons of the batter mixture into the pan and cook 5–6 fritters at a time for 3–4 minutes on each side until golden. Drain on kitchen paper and keep warm in a low oven while you cook the remaining fritters; it should make about 16 in total.

4. Meanwhile, mix together all the ingredients for the ponzu dipping sauce and season with pepper. Divide the sauce between four bowls and sprinkle with the remaining spring onion. Top the fritters with a handful of pea shoots and serve with the dipping sauce.

Serve with the Soba, Sea Vegetable and Radish Salad (see page 65).

Plump and sweet, young *peas* are delicious eaten straight from the pod or cooked lightly. Plant seeds outdoors in spring, in a sunny position. Plant taller growing plants in nutrient-rich soil in a single row, 5cm/2in deep, making sure there is enough room for cane supports. Dwarf plants can be sown in a round trench. Harvest the peas regularly or the plants will stop producing flowers and pods.

I prefer to mash the kidney beans to give a chunky texture to the bean cakes. You could use a stick blender or food processor for a smoother end result, but bear in mind that tinned beans are softer in texture than dried. The chipotle paste, made from smoked jalapeño chillies, is a favourite and adds a rich, smoky, spicy kick. To complement the Mexican feel, try serving the bean cakes with the Mexican Fattoush (see page 157).

Chipotle, Carrot & Red Bean Cakes

Serves: 4   *Preparation time:* 20 minutes   *Cooking time:* 12 minutes

480g/1lb 1oz/scant 2½ cups drained tinned
   red kidney beans or cooked dried beans
   (see pages 8–9)
1 large carrot, coarsely grated
3 garlic cloves, crushed
1 handful of micro sprouts, such as radish,
   alfalfa or broccoli
100g/3½oz/1½ cups fresh breadcrumbs
2–3 tbsp tomato ketchup, to taste
1–2 tbsp smoked chipotle paste, to taste

plain flour, for dusting
vegetable oil, for frying
1 large handful of coriander leaves,
   chopped, to serve

SWEET CHILLI AND LIME YOGURT
125ml/4fl oz/½ cup thick natural yogurt
juice of 1 lime
4 tbsp sweet chilli sauce, or to taste
sea salt and freshly ground black pepper

1. To make the sweet chilli and lime yogurt, mix together all the ingredients in a serving bowl and season with salt and pepper.

2. Mash the kidney beans with a fork or potato masher in a bowl to make a coarse paste. Stir in the carrot, garlic, micro sprouts, breadcrumbs, ketchup and chipotle paste. Season well with salt and pepper, then taste and add more chipotle if you like more of a kick. Alternatively, add an extra tablespoon of ketchup.

3. Dust a large plate with flour. Form the bean mixture into 12 patties (or 4 large burgers) about 1.5cm/⅝in thick. Dust lightly with flour, patting the patties to remove any excess.

4. Heat enough oil to cover the base of a large, non-stick frying pan over a medium heat. Fry the bean cakes in two batches for 3 minutes on each side, or until golden and crisp. Drain on kitchen paper and keep warm. Serve the bean cakes with the sweet chilli and lime yogurt, sprinkled with coriander.

Root vegetables cost little to buy and add nourishment and substance to this warming, filling pie.

Winter Root, Cheddar & Cider Pie

Serves: 4–6 *Preparation time:* 45 minutes, plus cooling
Cooking time: 50 minutes

4 turnips, diced
2 parsnips, diced
3 carrots, diced
175g/6oz celeriac, diced
1 tbsp vegetable bouillon powder
20g/¾oz butter
2 onions, chopped
200g/7oz chestnut mushrooms, sliced
4 garlic cloves, chopped
leaves of 6 thyme sprigs, or 1 tsp dried thyme

1 heaped tbsp chopped sage leaves,
　plus 3 large leaves
2 heaped tbsp plain flour, plus extra
　for dusting
200ml/7fl oz/scant 1 cup dry cider
1 tbsp Dijon mustard
150g/5½oz mature Cheddar cheese, grated
400g/14oz puff pastry
1 egg, beaten, to glaze
sea salt and freshly ground black pepper

1. Put the root vegetables in a large saucepan and just cover with water. Bring to the boil and stir in the bouillon powder. Turn the heat down, part-cover and simmer for 12–15 minutes until the vegetables are tender. Strain the vegetables, reserving the stock.

2. Meanwhile, melt the butter in a large frying pan over a medium-high heat and fry the onions for 8 minutes until softened. Add the mushrooms, garlic and herbs and cook for another 5 minutes. Sprinkle the flour over the top and stir continuously for another minute. Pour in the cider, stir to lift any bits from the bottom of the pan and cook for 2 minutes until thickened and reduced. Add the cooked root vegetables, 350ml/12fl oz/scant 1½ cups of the reserved stock and the mustard and stir until combined. Season the filling well with salt and pepper. Transfer the root vegetable mixture to a 25 × 29cm/10 × 11½in pie dish (or a 27cm/10¾in round dish). Stir in the cheese and leave to cool.

3. Preheat the oven to 200°C/400°F/Gas 6. Roll out the pastry on a lightly floured work surface until large enough to cover the pie dish with about 2.5cm/1in to spare. Cut a 1cm/½in wide strip from the edge. Wet the rim of the pie dish with water and top with the strip of pastry. Brush with more water and drape the remaining pastry on top. Press the edge of the pastry to seal, trim away any excess and crimp with your finger and thumb. Tap the edge of the pastry with the flat blade of a table knife. Prick the top of the pie to let the steam escape and brush the top with beaten egg. Arrange the sage leaves on top and brush with a little more egg. Bake for 30 minutes until risen and golden. Serve hot.

Saltado is a Peruvian one-pan dish with an Asian influence. Traditionally made with beef, this meat-free version features marinated cubes of tofu, new potatoes and red peppers in a herby, spicy tomato sauce.

Pepper and Tofu Saltado

Serves: 4   **Preparation time:** *20 minutes, plus 1 hour marinating*
Cooking time: *45 minutes*

6 tbsp dark soy sauce

3 heaped tsp hot chilli paste

400g/14oz firm tofu, drained, patted dry and
   cut into cubes

3 tbsp olive oil, plus extra if needed

450g/1lb new potatoes, peeled and cubed

2 large onions, chopped

2 large red peppers, deseeded and cut
   into chunks

4 large garlic cloves, crushed

2 tsp ground coriander

2 tsp ground cumin

1 tbsp white wine vinegar

550g/1lb 4oz tomatoes, skinned, deseeded
   and chopped

2 large handfuls of mint leaves, chopped

2 large handfuls of coriander leaves, chopped

1. Mix together 2 tablespoons of the soy sauce and 2 teaspoons of the chilli paste in a large, shallow dish. Add the tofu and turn until it is coated in the marinade. Leave to marinate for 1 hour.

2. Twenty minutes before the tofu is ready, heat the oil in a large, deep frying pan over a medium heat. Add the potatoes and fry for 16–18 minutes, turning regularly, until golden and crisp all over. Remove the potatoes with a slotted spoon and drain on kitchen paper. Add the tofu to the pan and cook for 10 minutes, turning occasionally, until golden all over. Remove from the pan and drain on kitchen paper.

3. Add more oil to the pan if needed, then add the onion and cook for 6 minutes until softened. Add the red peppers and cook for another 3 minutes until tender. While they are cooking, mix together the garlic, ground spices, vinegar and the remaining soy sauce and chilli paste, then add it to the pan with the tomatoes and 5 tablespoons water. Cook for 5 minutes, stirring regularly, until the tomatoes break down to make a sauce. Return the cooked potatoes and tofu to the pan with three-quarters of the herbs and heat through. Serve sprinkled with the remaining herbs.

A jar of harissa goes a long way in my kitchen. It's spooned into mayo to make a quick sauce, brushed over roasted vegetables and stirred into couscous or, as here, used as the base of a quick marinade. The mushroom burgers come topped with a slice of golden grilled halloumi and a spoonful of red pepper and cumin dressing.

Mushroom Burgers

Serves: 4   *Preparation time:* 10 minutes, plus 30 minutes marinating
Cooking time: 12 minutes

3 tbsp extra virgin olive oil
3 tsp harissa
1 tsp lemon juice
4 large, flat portobello or field mushrooms,
   stalks discarded
4 slices of halloumi, rinsed and patted dry
4 focaccia rolls, split in half
sea salt and freshly ground black pepper
green salad, to serve

RED PEPPER AND CUMIN DRESSING
2 tbsp extra virgin olive oil
½ large red pepper, deseeded and diced
1 large garlic clove, finely chopped
½ tsp cumin seeds
1 tbsp balsamic vinegar
2 heaped tbsp roughly chopped
   coriander leaves

1. Mix together the olive oil, harissa and lemon juice and season with salt and pepper. Brush the marinade generously over both sides of each mushroom and leave to marinate for 30 minutes.

2. Preheat the grill to medium-high, and make the red pepper and cumin dressing. Heat 1 tablespoon of the oil in a large frying pan over a medium heat. Add the red pepper and fry for 3 minutes until softened then add the garlic and cumin seeds and cook for another minute, stirring regularly. Remove from the heat and transfer to a small bowl. Stir in the remaining oil, balsamic vinegar and coriander, then season. Leave to one side.

3. Put the marinated mushrooms, gill sides down, on a sheet of foil. Fold in the edges to make a border and to keep in any juices. Grill for 5 minutes until softened, then turn over and grill for another minute. Turn the grill to high, place a slice of halloumi on top of each mushroom and grill for another 2–3 minutes until softened and golden in places.

4. Grill the focaccia at the same time as cooking the mushrooms until lightly toasted. To serve, put a halloumi-topped mushroom on the bottom half of each focaccia and top with a generous spoonful of the dressing. Spoon any of the juices from the grilled mushrooms over the other half of the focaccia and put on top of the mushrooms. Serve with a green salad.

Only *pick mushrooms* when you are absolutely sure what they are. Arm yourself with a guidebook or, even better, attend a course or go with a seasoned forager. The field mushroom is perhaps the most commonly eaten wild fungus. Find them in meadows, fields and pastureland from late summer into autumn. Take care when identifying them, as there are poisonous fungi that look very like them.

 ## Beetroot

Out of the many vegetables to choose from it may seem strange to pick beetroot, but its earthy, sweet flavour and vibrant magenta colour means it lends itself to so many savoury – and even sweet – dishes. Beetroot is a close relative of chard and spinach, so be sure not to waste the leaves, as they can be prepared and cooked in the same way. Bake the firm globes of beetroot whole (unpeeled to stop them bleeding) or reduce the roasting time by cutting them into wedges; either way they need to be cooked until tender and richly sweet. Alternatively, boil, pickle or grate raw into salads – and cakes! And then there's the stunning Italian candy-striped beetroot, also known as chioggia, with its concentric circles in varying shades of pink, red, yellow and white. It looks dramatic cut into paper-thin slices and served as part of a salad.

Adding beetroot to savoury or sweet muffins makes them wonderfully moist, in much the same way as adding carrots or courgettes does, and they also benefit from the vegetable's vibrant ruby colour. If using ready-cooked beetroot, make sure you buy the kind without any vinegar. Also, try to use a crumbly goats' cheese rather than a runny one for the best results. The secret to successful light muffins is to keep mixing to a minimum; briefly fold the ingredients together and you're done – they don't even have to be thoroughly combined.

Beetroot and Goats' Cheese Muffins

Makes: 12   **Preparation time:** 15 minutes   **Cooking time:** 25 minutes

sunflower oil, for greasing
280g/10oz/2¼ cups plain flour
½ tsp sea salt
2 tsp baking powder
½ tsp bicarbonate of soda
2 large eggs, lightly beaten

300ml/10½fl oz/scant 1¼ cups natural yogurt
85g/3oz butter, melted
115g/4oz goats' cheese, crumbled
225g/8oz cooked beetroot, coarsely grated
2 tbsp pumpkin seeds

1. Preheat the oven to 190°C/375°F/Gas 5. Lightly grease a 12-hole deep muffin tin with oil (or you could make 6 large muffins using large paper muffin cases).

2. Sift together the flour, salt, baking powder and bicarbonate of soda into a mixing bowl.

3. Mix together the eggs and yogurt and beat in the melted butter. Stir the dry ingredients into the wet ingredients, then gently fold in the goats' cheese and beetroot until just combined. Spoon the mixture into the prepared muffin tin, sprinkle with the pumpkin seeds and bake for 20–25 minutes, or until risen and golden.

Rather than waste the leftover egg whites, freeze them in a small plastic pot or ice cube tray. Save them up and use to make meringues or for the base of a tempura batter.

Pictured on page 171.

Beetroot Jam

A spoonful of this thick, sticky, earthy, savoury jam goes particularly well with robust-flavoured cheeses, or nut or bean-based dishes. Sauté **1 large finely chopped onion** in **1 tbsp olive oil** for 10 minutes until softened but not coloured. Add **2 (about 280g/10oz) peeled and grated raw beetroot**, **1 large peeled and grated apple**, **100ml/3½fl oz/scant ½ cup each of cider vinegar** and **water** and **4 tbsp soft brown sugar**. Stir well and bring up to boiling point, then turn the heat down to medium-low, part-cover the pan and simmer for 40 minutes until the beetroot is very tender. Remove the lid and simmer for 15 minutes, stirring now and then, to reduce the liquid in the pan and until the mixture is jam-like in consistency. Season with **salt** and **pepper** and leave the jam to cool before serving, or spoon into a sterilized jar (see page 11) and keep for up to 1 month.

Lebanese Beetroot Dip

This simple dip is delicious slathered onto warm flatbreads or scooped up with vegetables. I like to roast my own beetroot but you could use ready-cooked if time is short. Preheat the oven to 200°C/400°F/Gas 6. Trim **2 (about 280g/10oz) beetroot** and wrap them in foil. Roast for 1 hour– 1 hour 15 minutes until the beetroot can be easily pierced all the way through with a skewer. Leave until cool enough to handle, then peel away the skin and roughly chop. Blend the beetroot with **6 tbsp natural yogurt**, **the juice of ½ lemon**, **1 crushed garlic clove**, **1 chopped red chilli**, **2 tsp ras el hanout** and **½ tsp ground cumin** until smooth. Season well with **salt** and **pepper** and spoon the dip into a serving bowl. Serve scattered with **crumbled feta cheese** and **coriander** and **mint leaves**.

Roast Beetroot Crisps

Preheat the oven to 180°C/350°F/Gas 4. Thinly slice **5 raw beetroot** (they should be about 3mm/⅛in thick) using a mandolin or very sharp knife. Pat the beetroot slices dry with kitchen paper and lightly brush both sides with **olive oil**. Put in a single layer on two baking sheets and roast for 20–25 minutes, turning the beetroot once and swapping the trays around at the same time, until just crisp (they will crisp up more when cool). Keep an eye on the beetroot as they can burn easily in a matter of minutes. Drain on kitchen paper and season with **sea salt**.

Index

A

arancini eggs 68
Asian stock 15
Asian-style mash 22
asparagus, tagliatelle with 54
aubergines: aubergine meze 158
   spaghetti with aubergine, cheese
     and mint 49

B

barley, squash and wild oregano
    risotto 82
basil sauce 46
beans 8–9
beet top, spring onion and Gruyère
    tart 144
beetroot 170–3
   beetroot and goats' cheese
     muffins 172
   beetroot jam 173
   Lebanese beetroot dip 173
   roast beetroot crisps 173
bibimbap 75
black beans: black bean tostados 37
   Chinese black bean and mozzarella
     salad 151
   oriental black bean and mushroom
     broth 28
bread: broad bean and goats' cheese
    crostini 160
   cheese and pepper strata 143
   roasted panzanella 150
broad beans: broad bean and goats'
    cheese crostini 160
   last-of-the-beans risotto 81
bruschetta, polenta 86
buckwheat and sour cherry salad 71
buns, yum cha 98
burgers, mushroom 168
Burmese noodle, tofu and winter
    greens curry 64
   Spanish-style white beans 38

C

cabbage: mustard-soy greens 108
cashews, spiced 80
cheese: beet top, spring onion and
    Gruyère tart 144

beetroot and goats' cheese
   muffins 172
broad bean and goats' cheese
   crostini 160
cheese and pepper strata 143
cheesy chilli cornbread 87
Chinese black bean and mozzarella
   salad 151
courgette, feta and walnut
   cavatappi 50
Easter egg pies 120
feta and pumpkin seed pilaff 74
goats' cheese pancakes 138
homemade paneer 17
lentil sambar with paneer 139
mozzarella 148–51
mozzarella with Szechuan pepper
   151
pizzata 119
potted cheese 132
rainbow chard and Parmesan
   tortino 128
ricotta and wild greens dumplings
   140
scamorza, orzo and basil oil salad
   151
tandoori halloumi 135
twice-baked cheese soufflés 122
watermelon, feta and mint salad
   136
chestnut and mushroom pie 104
chillies: cheesy chilli cornbread 87
   chilaquiles 115
   chilli oil 52
   tomato and chilli salsa 22
Chinese black bean and mozzarella
   salad 151
Chinese leaves: kimchi 20
chipotle, carrot and red bean cakes
   164
chutney, mango 19
coconut and pineapple salad 135
coconut curry, Sri Lankan 103
conchiglie and broccoli gratin 147
cornbread, cheesy chilli 87
courgette, feta and walnut cavatappi
   50
curries 15, 64, 103

D

dukka 109
dumplings, ricotta and wild greens
   140

E

Easter egg pies 120
edamame and wasabi hummus 32
eggs: arancini eggs 68
   Easter egg pies 120
   eggah 129
   eggs with lemongrass cream 125
   Greek egg and lemon soup 112
   linguine carbonara 53
   omelettes 126
   pizzata 119
   rainbow chard and Parmesan
     tortino 128
   sous-vide omelette 129
   spiced baked eggs 118
   sushi rolls 129
   Tunisian eggs 116
elderflower syrup 25

F

fattoush, Mexican 157
fava bean purée 31
feta and pumpkin seed pilaff 74
fritters, pea and tofu 162

G

garlic 142
gnocchi, semolina and nut milk 96
grains 7
Greek egg and lemon soup 112
greens: Easter egg pies 120
   ricotta and wild greens dumplings
    140

H

hummus, endamame and wasabi 32

J

jam, beetroot 173

J

kale chips, pho with 60
kimchi 20

L

last-of-the-beans risotto 81
latkes, potato and parsnip 123
Lebanese beetroot dip 173
lemons, quick preserved 24
lentils 8–9
    lentil, preserved lemon and date
        tagine 34
    lentil sambar with paneer 139
    Puy lentil, squash and crispy
        chickpea salad 33
linguine carbonara 53

M

mangoes: mango chutney 19
    smoked tofu and mango salad 43
Mexican fattoush 157
Moroccan slow-cooked vegetables
    159
mozzarella 148–51
muffins, beetroot and goats' cheese
    172
mushrooms: chestnut and mushroom
    pie 104
    creamy porcini and sea beet orzo
        57
    mushroom burgers 168
    oriental black bean and mushroom
        broth 28
    roasted mushrooms with couscous
        crust 79
    yum cha buns 98

N

noodles 8, 62–5
    Burmese noodle, tofu and winter
        greens curry 64
    pho with kale chips 60
    soba, sea vegetable and radish
        salad 65
    soba with coriander dressing 65
    soba with miso sauce 65
    tempeh with peanut sauce 102
    udon noodle pot with tahini and
        wild garlic 58
nuts: nut stuffing 101
    roasted nuts 18
    tamari nuts and seeds 109

O

omelettes 126–9
onions: crispy onions and ginger 23
    roasted onions with nut stuffing
        101
oriental black bean and mushroom
    broth 28
orzo, creamy porcini and sea beet 57

P

paella with poor man's saffron 76
pancakes, goats' cheese 138
paneer 17
    lentil sambar with 139
panzanella, roasted 150
parsnips: potato and parsnip latkes
    123
pasta 8
    conchiglie and broccoli gratin 147
    courgette, feta and walnut
        cavatappi 50
    creamy porcini and sea beet orzo
        57
    linguine carbonara with crispy
        capers 53
    rigatoni with golden lemon crumbs
        52
    scamorza, orzo and basil oil salad
        151
    spaghetti with aubergine, cheese
        and mint 49
    tagliatelle with asparagus and
        wild garlic pesto 54
    wonton ravioli with rocket 59
pastry 13, 104
pea and tofu fritters 162
peanuts: quinoa and roasted peanut
    salad 72
    tempeh with peanut sauce 102
pears: elderflower pears 132
    pecan, pear and nasturtium salad
        94
pecan, pear and nasturtium salad 94
peppers: cheese and pepper strata
    143
    pepper and tofu saltado 167
pesto, wild garlic 54
pho with kale chips 60

pies 104, 120, 165
pilaff, feta and pumpkin seed 74
pineapple: coconut and pineapple
    salad 135
pizzata 119
polenta 84–7
pomegranate salsa 21
potatoes: Asian-style mash 22
    pepper and tofu saltado 167
    pizzata 119
    potato and borage salad 154
    potato and parsnip latkes 123
Provençal soup 46
pumpkin seed rolls 97
Puy lentil, squash and crispy chickpea
    salad 33

Q

quinoa and roasted peanut salad 72

R

rainbow chard and Parmesan tortino
    128
ravioli, wonton 59
rice 7
    arancini eggs 68
    bibimbap 75
    last-of-the-beans risotto 81
    paella with poor man's saffron
        76
    sesame and nori cakes 108
    sushi rolls 129
    Thai rice with spiced cashews 80
ricotta and wild greens dumplings
    140
rigatoni with golden lemon crumbs 52
risotto 81, 82

S

salads: buckwheat and sour cherry 71
    Chinese black bean and mozzarella
        151
    coconut and pineapple 135
    Mexican fattoush 157
    mozzarella with Szechuan pepper
        151
    pecan, pear and nasturtium 94
    potato and borage 154

Puy lentil, squash and crispy
    chickpea 33
quinoa and roasted peanut 72
roasted panzanella 150
scamorza, orzo and basil oil 151
sesame, orange and dandelion 109
smoked tofu and mango 43
soba, sea vegetable and radish 65
toasted walnut 93
watermelon, feta and mint 136
salsas 21, 22
scamorza, orzo and basil oil salad 151
sea beet: creamy porcini and sea
    beet orzo 57
seeds: roasted seeds 18
    tamari nuts and seeds 109
semolina and nut milk gnocchi 96
sesame seeds 106–9
    dukka 109
    sesame and nori cakes 108
    sesame, orange and dandelion
        salad 109
shortcrust pastry 13
soba noodles see noodles
soufflés, twice-baked cheese 122
soups: Greek egg and lemon soup 112
    oriental black bean and mushroom
        broth 28
    pho with kale chips 60

Provençal soup 46
spaghetti with aubergine, cheese
    and mint 49
Spanish-style white beans 38
spring onions 114
squash: barley, squash and wild
    oregano risotto 82
    Puy lentil, squash and crispy
        chickpea salad 33
    tahini and squash dip 90
Sri Lankan coconut curry 103
stocks 14–15
suet pastry 104
sushi rolls 129
sweet potatoes: Asian-style mash 22

T
tagliatelle with asparagus 54
tahini and squash dip 90
tamari nuts and seeds 109
tandoori halloumi 135
tarts 87, 144
tempeh with peanut sauce 102
Thai rice with spiced cashews 80
tofu 40–3
    Burmese noodle, tofu and winter
        greens curry 64
    crispy Thai spiced tofu 43
    pea and tofu fritters 162

pepper and tofu saltado 167
smoked tofu and mango salad 43
tofu bahn mi 43
tofu escalopes with salsa 42
tomatoes: tomato and chilli salsa 22
    tomato sauce 140
tortillas 37, 115
Tunisian eggs 116

V
vegetables: Moroccan slow-cooked
    vegetables 159
vegetable stock 14
see also peppers; tomatoes etc

W
walnuts: toasted walnut salad 93
wasabi: endamame and wasabi
    hummus 32
watermelon, feta and mint salad 136
wild garlic: udon noodle pot with 58
    wild garlic pesto 54
winter root, Cheddar and cider pie
    165
wonton ravioli 59

Y
yogurt, wholemilk 16
yum cha buns 98

ACKNOWLEDGEMENTS

My heartfelt thanks go to Grace Cheetham, for her ongoing support, encouragement and belief in me. It has – as always – been an utmost pleasure to work with the dedicated team at Nourish, especially Rebecca Woods and Suzanne Tuhrim, who have been fantastic. I would also like to thank my freelance editor, Liz Jones. Thanks, too, to Jayne Cross who prepared the food for photography and brought the recipes to life, as did the talented (and funny) photographer, Toby Scott, and stylist Lucy Harvey. It was great to work with you all. I would also like to thank Silvio, Ella and Joel for putting up with the mess I always seem to make – and for happily tasting my creations, even late into the evening!

NOURISH
EAT WELL, LIVE WELL

Few things in life are as important as what you eat.
If you've enjoyed this book and want to read more about wholesome and healthy food,
please visit us at **www.nourishbooks.com**